101 Things®
To Do With
Pumpkin

101 Things To Do With Pumpkin

BY
ELIZA CROSS

GIBBS SMITH
TO ENRICH AND INSPIRE HUMANKIND

First Edition
19 18 17 16 15   5 4 3 2

Text © 2015 Eliza Cross

101 Things is a registered trademark of Gibbs Smith,
Publisher and Stephanie Ashcraft.

Published by
Gibbs Smith
P.O. Box 667
Layton, Utah 84041

1.800.835.4993 orders
www.gibbs-smith.com

Printed and bound in Korea
Gibbs Smith books are printed on either recycled, 100% post-consumer
waste, FSC-certified papers or on paper produced from sustainable PEFC-
certified forest/controlled wood source. Learn more at www.pefc.org.

Library of Congress Cataloging-in-Publication Data

Cross, Eliza.
  101 things to do with pumpkin / Eliza Cross. — First edition.
      pages cm
  ISBN 978-1-4236-4083-7
1. Cooking (Pumpkin) I. Title. II. Title: One hundred and one things to
do with pumpkin. III. Title: One hundred one things to do with pumpkin.
  TX803.P93C76 2015
  641.6'562—dc23

                                                          2015014565

For my sweet son, Michael Castaneda.

Yum!

**More recipes and tips
at 101yum.com**

CONTENTS

Soups and Stews

Autumn Stew in a Pumpkin 58 • Creamy Pumpkin Carrot Soup 59 • Slow-Cooked Pumpkin Chili 60 • Curried Pumpkin Soup 61 • Pumpkin and Black Bean Soup 62 • Comforting Pumpkin Chicken Soup 63 • Pumpkin Potato Soup 64 • Pumpkin, Corn, and Shrimp Bisque 65 • Pumpkin Tortilla Soup 66

Side Dishes

Pumpkin Fries with Honey Mustard 68 • Pumpkin Mashed Potatoes 69 • Roasted Pumpkin and Acorn Squash 70 • Pumpkin Spoon Bread 71 • Crispy Pumpkin Potato Bake 72 • Maple Roasted Pumpkin and Brussels Sprouts 73 • Pumpkin Fritters 74 • Cauliflower Pumpkin Gratin 75

Dinners

Glazed Pumpkin BBQ Meatloaf 78 • Pumpkin Ravioli 79 • Pumpkin Bacon Broccoli Pasta 80 • Pumpkin Apple Pecan Chicken 81 • Autumn Lasagna 82 • Pumpkin Risotto 83 • Pumpkin Turkey Enchiladas 84 • Hearty Pumpkin Shepherd's Pie 85 • Roast Pumpkin, Sausage, and Caramelized Onion Pizza 86 • Creamy Pumpkin Mac and Cheese 87

Desserts

Perfect Pumpkin Pie 90 • Deep Dish Pumpkin Custard Pie 91 • Pumpkin Chiffon Pie 92 • Pumpkin Cream Pie 93 • No-Bake Pumpkin Caramel Cream Pie 94 • Pumpkin Praline Ice Cream Pie 95 • Pumpkin Crunch Cheesecake 96 • Decadent Pumpkin Butter Cake 97 • Pumpkin Roll 98 • Pumpkin Dump Cake 99 • Pumpkin Pound Cake 100 • Pumpkin Crumb Cake 101 • Pumpkin Chocolate Chip Cake 102 • Creamy Pumpkin Tiramisu 103 • Pumpkin Apple Crisp 104 • Pumpkin Cream Puffs 105 • Pumpkin Bread Pudding 106 • Luscious Layered Pumpkin Dessert 107 • Mini Pumpkin Turnovers 108

Cookies and Bars

Pumpkin Chocolate Chip Cookies 110 • Maple-Glazed Pumpkin Oatmeal Cookies 111 • Pumpkin Snickerdoodles 112 • Pumpkin Toffee Blondies 113 • Pumpkin Gingersnaps 114 • Pumpkin Shortbread Cookies 115 • Pumpkin Mini Whoopie Pies 116 • Pumpkin Ginger 6-Layer Bars 117 • Pumpkin Bars with Cream Cheese Frosting 118 • Pumpkin Pecan Pie Bars 119 • Pumpkin Chocolate Swirl Brownies 120 • Pumpkin Granola Bars 121 • Pumpkin Angel Bars 122 • Pumpkin Biscotti 123 • Pumpkin Butterscotch Cookies 124

HELPFUL HINTS

1. When picking out a pumpkin for cooking, look for smaller pie pumpkin varieties which are sweeter and smoother-textured than those grown for carving Jack-o-lanterns.

2. Select a firm, unbruised pumpkin with consistent color and a sturdy stem; be sure to check the bottom of the pumpkin to make sure the base is undamaged.

3. Shake the pumpkin and avoid it if you can hear liquid sloshing inside. Smell the pumpkin; it should have a fresh, clean aroma.

4. To avoid breakage, always lift and carry a pumpkin from underneath rather than by the stem, which can become dried and snap off.

5. Always scrub the outside of a pumpkin with warm water and a vegetable brush before cooking.

6. Use a metal ice cream scoop, serrated grapefruit spoon, or melon baller to remove the stringy pulp from inside a pumpkin.

7. When hollowing out a large pumpkin, avoid getting messy by scraping around the sides starting from the hole opening and working your way down to the bottom.

8. One 8-inch diameter pie pumpkin will yield about 3 cups of cooked, mashed pumpkin.

9. Pumpkin seeds can be roasted and eaten in their hulls; see recipe for "Roasted Pumpkin Seeds" in the Basic Recipes section.

10. Pepitas are hulled green pumpkin seeds that are sometimes called for in Mexican recipes. Removing the hulls from seeds can be tedious

work, but raw pepitas can often be found in Latin American markets and natural foods stores.

11. When using canned pumpkin, look for cans labeled "solid-pack" rather than "pumpkin pie filling," which has added ingredients.

12. If you don't have pumpkin pie spice on hand, substitute $1/2$ teaspoon cinnamon, $1/4$ teaspoon ginger, $1/8$ teaspoon nutmeg, $1/8$ teaspoon allspice, and a pinch of cloves for each teaspoon.

13. If your pumpkin puree is too watery, line a strainer or sieve with cheesecloth and put it inside a larger bowl. Pour in the puree, cover with plastic wrap, and refrigerate while draining away the excess liquid.

14. Leftover cooked pumpkin puree freezes well; wrap tightly and use within 9 months for best quality.

15. Firm, unbruised pumpkins can be stored in a cool, dry place for 1 month.

16. Butternut squash can be substituted for pumpkin. Some brands of commercial canned pumpkin are actually produced from a butternut squash variety.

BASIC
RECIPES

OVEN-COOKED PUMPKIN PUREE

 1 **medium pie pumpkin,** about 4 pounds
 $1/2$ cup **water**

Preheat oven to 350 degrees.

Wash the pumpkin and cut out the top and stem with a sharp knife.
Lay on a cutting board and carefully cut in half. Scrape out stringy pulp
and seeds. (Rinse and reserve seeds to make Roasted Pumpkin Seeds, if
desired.)

Cut pumpkin in large pieces and arrange skin-side up in a roasting pan.
Pour water in the bottom of the pan and cover with aluminum foil.
Bake 45–60 minutes, or until pumpkin is soft and easily pierced with a
fork. Cool to room temperature.

Scrape the soft pulp from the skin into a food processor or heavy-
duty blender, discarding the skin. Pulse until evenly pureed, adding
a little water if necessary to make a smooth puree. Alternately, mash
the pulp in a large bowl with a potato masher or run it through a food
mill. If finished puree is too watery, drain in a fine mesh strainer for
30 minutes.

The puree can be used immediately or refrigerated, covered, and used
within 3 days. The puree may also be frozen, tightly wrapped, or stored
in an airtight container for up to 6 months. Makes about 8 cups.

STEAMED PUMPKIN PUREE

1 **small pie pumpkin,** about 2 pounds
1 cup **water**

Wash the pumpkin and cut out the top and stem with a sharp knife. Lay on a cutting board and carefully cut in half. Scrape out stringy pulp and seeds. (Rinse and reserve seeds to make Roasted Pumpkin Seeds, if desired.) Cut pumpkin in 4-inch pieces.

Stovetop steaming method: In a large pot fitted with a steamer basket, heat water to boiling. Add the pumpkin, reduce heat to a simmer, and cover. Cook until pumpkin is tender, about 30 minutes. Drain and cool to room temperature.

Microwave steaming method: Place the pumpkin pieces in a microwave-safe bowl, add the water, cover, and cook on high until pumpkin is fork tender, about 15–20 minutes depending on microwave. Cool to room temperature.

Scrape the soft pulp from the skin into a food processor or heavy-duty blender, discarding the skin. Pulse until evenly pureed, adding a little water if necessary to make a smooth puree. Alternately, mash the pulp in a large bowl with a potato masher or run it through a food mill. If finished puree is too watery, drain in a fine mesh strainer for 30 minutes.

The puree can be used immediately or refrigerated, covered, and used within 3 days. The puree may also be frozen, tightly wrapped, or stored in an airtight container for up to 6 months. Makes about 4 cups.

SLOW COOKER PUMPKIN PUREE

| 1 | **small pie pumpkin,** about 2 pounds |
| ¹/₄ cup | **water** |

Wash the pumpkin and cut out the top and stem with a sharp knife. Lay on a cutting board and carefully cut in half. Scrape out stringy pulp and seeds. (Rinse and reserve seeds to make Roasted Pumpkin Seeds, if desired.) Cut pumpkin in pieces, place in a 3-quart slow cooker, and cook on low for 4–6 hours, or until skin is soft and easy to pierce with a fork. Cool to room temperature.

Scrape the soft pulp from the skin into a food processor or heavy-duty blender, discarding the skin. Pulse until evenly pureed, adding a little of the cooking water if necessary to make a smooth puree. Alternately, mash the pulp in a large bowl with a potato masher or run it through a food mill. If finished puree is too watery, drain in a fine mesh strainer for 30 minutes.

The puree can be used immediately or refrigerated, covered, and used within 3 days. The puree may also be frozen, tightly wrapped, or stored in an airtight container for up to 6 months. Makes about 4 cups.

PUMPKIN PIE SPICE

$^1/_3$ cup **cinnamon**
1 tablespoon **ginger**
1 tablespoon **nutmeg or mace**
1 $^1/_2$ teaspoons **cloves**
1 $^1/_2$ teaspoons **allspice**

Place all the ingredients in a small jar with a tight-fitting lid and shake to combine. For a single 9-inch pumpkin pie, add 1–1 $^1/_2$ teaspoons spice mix to recipe. Makes about $^1/_2$ cup.

ROASTED PUMPKIN SEEDS

2 cups	**pumpkin seeds**
8 cups	**water**
2 tablespoons plus 1 teaspoon	**salt,** divided
2 tablespoons	**olive oil**
$1/2$ teaspoon	**pepper**
$1/4$ teaspoon	**cayenne pepper**

Preheat oven to 400 degrees.

Combine the pumpkin seeds, water, and 2 tablespoons salt in a large saucepan and bring to a boil over medium-high heat. Reduce heat and simmer for 10 minutes. Remove from heat and drain in a strainer. Spread the seeds on paper towels and blot to dry. Transfer to a large bowl and drizzle with the olive oil. Sprinkle in remaining 1 teaspoon salt, pepper, and cayenne pepper; toss to combine.

Spread the seeds evenly on a heavy, rimmed baking sheet and roast until lightly browned, for about 18–20 minutes, stirring once halfway during cooking. Remove from oven and cool on the pan to room temperature. Makes 4 servings.

Variation: After drizzling boiled, drained seeds with olive oil, sprinkle with 2 teaspoons Worcestershire sauce, 2 teaspoons soy sauce and $1/2$ teaspoon garlic powder in addition to salt, pepper, and cayenne pepper. Proceed as above.

BEVERAGES AND SWEETS

PUMPKIN SPICE LATTE

3 1/2 cups	**milk**
1/2 cup	**canned or cooked pumpkin puree**
1/4 cup	**sugar**
1 tablespoon	**vanilla**
1 teaspoon	**pumpkin pie spice**
1 1/2 cups	**strong coffee or espresso**
	whipped cream

In a large saucepan over medium heat, combine the milk, pumpkin, sugar, vanilla, and pie spice. Heat, stirring constantly, until sugar dissolves. Add the coffee or espresso and heat just until small bubbles form around the edge of the pan. Divide among 4 large coffee mugs and garnish with whipped cream. Makes 4 servings.

PUMPKIN HOT CHOCOLATE

3 cups	**milk**
I cup	**canned or cooked pumpkin puree**
I teaspoon	**pumpkin pie spice**
I teaspoon	**vanilla**
1/8 teaspoon	**salt**
4 ounces	**milk chocolate,** chopped
	whipped cream
	caramel syrup

In a medium saucepan over medium heat, combine the milk, pumpkin, pie spice, vanilla, and salt. Cook, stirring constantly, just until the mixture begins to simmer. Add the chocolate and cook, stirring constantly, until chocolate melts. Transfer to a blender or food processor and process until mixture is completely smooth. Divide among 4 mugs, top with whipped cream, and drizzle with caramel syrup. Makes 4 servings.

CREAMY PUMPKIN SMOOTHIES

2 cups	**vanilla yogurt**
1 1/2 cups	**canned or cooked pumpkin puree,** chilled
2/3 cup	**orange juice**
1 tablespoon	**sugar**
1 teaspoon	**cinnamon**
1/2 teaspoon	**pumpkin pie spice,** plus extra for garnish
1 cup	**ice cubes**
2	**small ripe bananas,** sliced

Combine yogurt, pumpkin, orange juice, sugar, cinnamon, and pie spice in a food processor or blender, and process until smooth, about 10 seconds. Add ice cubes and bananas and process until smooth, about 40–60 seconds. Divide among 4 glasses and garnish with a dash of pie spice. Makes 4 servings.

PUMPKIN PIE MILKSHAKES

8	**vanilla wafer cookies**
1/2 teaspoon	**cinnamon**
1/4 teaspoon	**nutmeg**
I pint	**vanilla ice cream,** softened
1 1/3 cups	**milk**
2/3 cup	**canned or cooked pumpkin puree,** chilled
	whipped cream

Place the cookies, cinnamon, and nutmeg in a blender or food processor and pulse until mixture is finely ground. Add the ice cream, milk, and pumpkin; blend until smooth. Serve in chilled glasses topped with whipped cream. Makes 4 servings.

PUMPKIN SPICED CIDER

1 cup	**canned or cooked pumpkin puree**
3 cups	**apple cider**
1/2 cup	**water**
1 1/2 teaspoons	**pumpkin pie spice**
4	**cinnamon sticks**

In a large saucepan, mix together the pumpkin, cider, water, pie spice, and cinnamon. Bring mixture to a boil. Reduce heat to low and simmer for 20 minutes. If mixture seems too thick, add additional cider.

Strain the mixture through a mesh strainer and reserve cinnamon sticks. Pour in warm cups and garnish with cinnamon sticks. Makes 4 servings.

PUMPKIN FUDGE

2 cups	**sugar**
I cup	**packed light brown sugar**
³/₄ cup	**butter**
I can (5 ounces)	**evaporated milk**
¹/₂ cup	**canned or cooked pumpkin puree**
2 teaspoons	**pumpkin pie spice**
I package (12 ounces)	**white chocolate chips**
I jar (7 ounces)	**marshmallow creme**
I ¹/₂ teaspoons	**vanilla**

Line the bottom and sides of a 9 x 13-inch baking pan with aluminum foil, and prepare with nonstick cooking spray; reserve.

In a medium, heavy-bottomed saucepan over medium heat, combine the sugar, brown sugar, butter, milk, pumpkin, and pie spice. Bring to a full rolling boil, stirring constantly. Continue boiling, stirring constantly, until candy thermometer reaches the soft-ball stage, 234 degrees, about 10–12 minutes.

Remove from heat and quickly stir in chocolate chips, marshmallow creme, and vanilla. Stir until chocolate is completely melted, and immediately pour into prepared pan. Cool pan on wire rack to room temperature, and then cover and chill in the refrigerator for 3 hours. Remove foil and cut in 1-inch squares. Makes about 2³/₄ pounds.

PUMPKIN WHITE CHOCOLATE TRUFFLES

1 pound	**white chocolate,** chopped, divided
2/3 cup	**canned or cooked pumpkin puree**
1/2 cup	**cream cheese,** softened
1 teaspoon	**pumpkin pie spice**
1 1/3 cups	**finely-crushed graham cracker crumbs**

Line a baking sheet with parchment paper and reserve.

In a small saucepan, melt 1/4 pound of chocolate over medium-low heat. Transfer to a medium bowl and add the pumpkin, cream cheese, and pie spice. Stir until mixture is smooth. Add the graham cracker crumbs and stir until well blended. Cover and refrigerate for 30 minutes.

Remove bowl from refrigerator and roll the mixture into 1-inch balls. Arrange on prepared baking sheet and place in the freezer for 30 minutes.

Melt the remaining 3/4 pound of chocolate in a saucepan over medium-low heat. Remove from heat and cool for 5 minutes. Remove the truffles from the freezer and using a fork, dip each one evenly in the melted chocolate, tapping excess chocolate off and arranging on the baking sheet. Return to the freezer for 10 minutes before serving. Makes about 36 truffles.

PUMPKIN CREAM CHOCOLATE CUPS

2 cups	**milk chocolate chips**
$1/2$ cup	**canned or cooked pumpkin puree**
4 ounces	**cream cheese,** softened
$1/4$ cup	**sugar**
1 teaspoon	**pumpkin pie spice**
$1/8$ teaspoon	**salt**

Line a mini muffin pan with 18 small paper candy cups.

Melt the chocolate chips in a saucepan over medium-low heat. Remove from heat and cool. Reserve.

In a small bowl, combine the pumpkin, cream cheese, sugar, pie spice, and salt; stir until smooth. Reserve.

Spoon 1 scant tablespoon of melted chocolate into a paper candy cup. Use the back of a teaspoon to spread the chocolate so that it coats the entire cup. Repeat with remaining cups and refrigerate for 10 minutes. Fill each cup half-full of the pumpkin mixture, using a spoon to level. Spoon melted chocolate on top of each cup so that it completely covers the surface, smoothing with a spoon if necessary. You may have chocolate or filling left over. Refrigerate until chocolate is firm, 2–3 hours. Store in refrigerator. Makes about 18 cups.

MUFFINS AND BREADS

PUMPKIN CREAM MUFFINS

2 1/2 cups	**sugar,** divided
2 1/2 cups	**flour,** divided
1/4 cup	**roughly chopped pecans**
3 tablespoons	**butter or margarine,** melted
2 1/2 teaspoons	**cinnamon,** divided
8 ounces	**cream cheese,** softened
3	**eggs**
1/2 teaspoon	**salt**
2 teaspoons	**baking powder**
1/4 teaspoon	**baking soda**
1 1/4 cups	**canned or cooked pumpkin puree**
1/3 cup	**vegetable oil**
1/2 teaspoon	**vanilla**

Preheat oven to 375 degrees and prepare two 12-cup muffin tins with nonstick cooking spray.

Combine 5 tablespoons sugar, 1/2 cup flour, pecans, butter, and 1/2 teaspoon cinnamon together in a medium bowl and reserve. In a separate medium bowl, beat together the cream cheese, 1 egg, and 3 tablespoons sugar in a small bowl and reserve.

In a large bowl, combine 2 cups sugar, 2 cups flour, salt, baking powder, baking soda, and 2 teaspoons cinnamon. Lightly beat 2 eggs, pumpkin, oil, and vanilla together in a medium bowl. Add the pumpkin mixture to the flour mixture and stir just until combined.

Evenly divide half of the batter among the muffin cups. Spoon 2 teaspoons of cream cheese mixture in the middle of each cup and top with the remaining batter. Sprinkle pecan mixture evenly over top and bake until golden, and a toothpick inserted in the center comes out clean, about 20–25 minutes. Cool on wire racks. Makes 24 muffins.

PUMPKIN SPICE SCONES

2 cups	**flour**
1/3 cup	**packed dark brown sugar**
1 1/4 teaspoons	**cinnamon,** divided
1 teaspoon	**baking powder**
3/4 teaspoon	**ginger,** divided
3/4 teaspoon	**cloves**
1/2 teaspoon	**nutmeg**
1/2 teaspoon	**baking soda**
1/4 teaspoon	**salt**
1/2 cup	**cold butter or margarine**
1/2 cup	**canned or cooked pumpkin puree**
5 tablespoons	**milk,** divided
1	**egg,** lightly beaten
2 teaspoons	**vanilla**
1 cup	**powdered sugar**

Preheat oven to 400 degrees and line a baking sheet with parchment paper. In a large bowl, combine flour, brown sugar, 1 teaspoon cinnamon, baking powder, 1/2 teaspoon ginger, cloves, nutmeg, baking soda, and salt. Cut in butter until mixture resembles coarse crumbs. In a large bowl, whisk together pumpkin, 3 tablespoons milk, egg, and vanilla. Add to flour mixture and stir just until a soft dough forms. Knead the dough 3–4 times on a lightly floured surface and roll in a 7 x 10-inch rectangle, about 1-inch thick. Cut in half lengthwise and crosswise to make 4 rectangles, and cut those in half diagonally to make 8 triangles. Transfer to prepared baking sheet. Bake for 10–12 minutes, or until edges are lightly browned and a toothpick inserted in the center comes out clean. Cool on a wire rack for 10 minutes.

In a small bowl, whisk together powdered sugar, 1/4 teaspoon cinnamon, 1/4 teaspoon ginger, and 2 tablespoons milk. Drizzle glaze over scones and allow to set before serving. Makes 8 servings.

PUMPKIN CINNAMON MINI MUFFINS

1 3/4 cups	**flour**
1 1/2 teaspoons	**baking powder**
1/2 teaspoon	**salt**
2 tablespoons plus 1 teaspoon	**cinnamon,** divided
1 teaspoon	**pumpkin pie spice**
1/2 teaspoon	**nutmeg**
1/2 cup	**butter or margarine,** melted, divided
1/2 cup	**packed dark brown sugar**
1	**egg**
3/4 cup	**canned or cooked pumpkin puree**
1/2 cup	**milk**
1 1/2 teaspoons	**vanilla**
1/2 cup	**sugar**

Preheat oven to 350 degrees and prepare a mini muffin tin with nonstick cooking spray.

In a large bowl, combine the flour, baking powder, salt, 1 teaspoon cinnamon, pie spice, and nutmeg; reserve. In a medium bowl, combine 1/4 cup melted butter, brown sugar, and egg; whisk until completely combined. Add the pumpkin, milk, and vanilla; whisk until well blended. Add to the flour mixture and stir until just combined; do not overmix. Spoon the batter into prepared muffin tins, about 2/3 full. Bake until lightly browned and a toothpick inserted in the center comes out clean, about 11–12 minutes. Cool to room temperature.

Combine the sugar and 2 tablespoons cinnamon in a small dish; pour 1/4 cup melted butter in another small dish. Dip the muffins in the melted butter and then in the cinnamon sugar, turning to coat. Makes about 24 mini muffins.

EASY 5-INGREDIENT PUMPKIN MUFFINS

I box (18 ounces)	**yellow cake mix**
I can (15 ounces) or 1 $^7/_8$ cups	**cooked pumpkin puree**
$^1/_2$ cup	**water**
I	**egg**
2 teaspoons	**pumpkin pie spice**

Preheat oven to 350 degrees and prepare two 12-cup muffin tins with nonstick cooking spray, or use paper liners.

In a large bowl, combine the cake mix, pumpkin, water, egg, and pie spice; beat with an electric mixer for I minute until combined. Pour the mixture in prepared muffin cups, about $^2/_3$ full. Bake for 20–25 minutes, or until a toothpick inserted in the center comes out clean. Makes 24 muffins.

PUMPKIN APPLE CRUNCH MUFFINS

2 1/2 cups plus 2 tablespoons	**flour,** divided
2 1/4 cups	**sugar,** divided
1 tablespoon	**pumpkin pie spice**
1 teaspoon	**baking soda**
1/2 teaspoon	**salt**
2	**eggs,** lightly beaten
1 cup	**canned or cooked pumpkin puree**
1/2 cup	**vegetable oil**
2 cups	**peeled, cored and chopped apples**
1/2 teaspoon	**cinnamon**
1 tablespoon	**cold butter or margarine**

Preheat oven to 350 degrees and prepare 18 muffin cups with nonstick cooking spray, or use paper liners.

In a large bowl, whisk together 2 1/2 cups flour, 2 cups sugar, pie spice, baking soda, and salt. In a medium bowl, whisk together eggs, pumpkin, and oil. Add pumpkin mixture to flour mixture, stirring just until blended. Fold in apples. Spoon batter into prepared muffin cups.

In a small bowl, mix together 2 tablespoons flour, 1/4 cup sugar, and cinnamon. Cut in butter until mixture resembles coarse crumbs. Sprinkle topping evenly over muffin batter. Bake for 35–40 minutes, or until a toothpick inserted in the center comes out clean. Makes 18 muffins.

PUMPKIN CARAMEL CINNAMON ROLLS

1 can (8 ounces)	**seamless croissant dough sheet**
1/3 cup	**canned or cooked pumpkin puree**
6 tablespoons	**butter or margarine,** softened, divided
1/4 cup plus 2 tablespoons	**packed dark brown sugar,** divided
2 tablespoons	**milk,** divided
1 teaspoon	**pumpkin pie spice**
1/4 teaspoon	**salt**
1/4 cup	**finely chopped pecans**
1/4 teaspoon	**vanilla**
1/4–1/3 cup	**powdered sugar**

Preheat oven to 350 degrees and prepare a 9-inch round cake pan with nonstick cooking spray.

Unroll dough and pat into a large rectangle. In a small bowl, combine pumpkin, 4 tablespoons butter, 2 tablespoons brown sugar, 1 tablespoon milk, pie spice, and salt; stir until well blended. Spread mixture over the dough and sprinkle with pecans. Starting with long side, roll up; pinch seam to seal. Cut in 12 equal slices and arrange cut side up in prepared pan. Bake 20–25 minutes, or until rolls are golden brown. Cool in pan on wire rack for 15 minutes.

Heat 2 tablespoons butter in a small saucepan until melted. Stir in 1/4 cup brown sugar and 1 tablespoon milk; cook over medium-low heat 1 minute. Cool for 5 minutes. Stir in vanilla and 1/4 cup powdered sugar and beat until well blended, adding more powdered sugar if needed until desired consistency is reached. Drizzle rolls with icing. Makes 12 servings.

PUMPKIN CHEESECAKE CRESCENTS

1/4 cup	**sugar**
1 teaspoon	**cinnamon**
1/3 cup plus 2 tablespoons	**cream cheese,** softened, divided
1 1/2 cups	**powdered sugar,** divided
1/4 cup	**canned or cooked pumpkin puree**
1/2 teaspoon	**pumpkin pie spice**
2 tubes (8 ounces each)	**refrigerated crescent rolls**
1 tablespoon	**butter or margarine,** melted
1 tablespoon	**milk**

Preheat oven to 375 degrees and line two baking sheets with parchment paper.

Combine the sugar and cinnamon in a small bowl; reserve.

In a medium bowl, combine 1/3 cup cream cheese, 1/2 cup powdered sugar, pumpkin, and pie spice. Beat with an electric mixer for 2–3 minutes, until smooth.

Unroll the crescents into 16 triangles. Spread a rounded tablespoon of the pumpkin mixture in the center of each triangle. Roll up in crescents and arrange on prepared baking sheet. Bake for 11–13 minutes, or until golden brown. Remove from oven, brush with melted butter while still hot, and sprinkle evenly with cinnamon sugar mixture. Cool to room temperature.

In a small bowl, combine 2 tablespoons cream cheese, 1 cup powdered sugar, and milk. Stir until well blended, adding extra milk if needed. Drizzle over crescents. Makes 16 servings.

PUMPKIN BISCUITS

1 ³/₄ cups	**flour**
¹/₄ cup	**packed light brown sugar**
2 ¹/₂ teaspoons	**baking powder**
¹/₂ teaspoon	**salt**
¹/₄ teaspoon	**baking soda**
¹/₂ cup plus 1 tablespoon	**cold butter or margarine,** divided
¹/₄ cup	**canned or cooked pumpkin puree**
¹/₃ cup	**buttermilk**

Preheat oven to 425 degrees and prepare a baking sheet with nonstick cooking spray.

In a large bowl, combine the flour, sugar, baking powder, salt, and baking soda. Cut in ¹/₂ cup butter until mixture resembles coarse crumbs. In a small bowl, combine pumpkin and buttermilk until well blended; add to flour mixture and stir just until moistened.

Turn dough onto a lightly floured surface, and knead 8–10 times. Roll or pat the dough into a rectangle about ³/₄-inch thick. Use a sharp knife to cut in 12 squares, and arrange each biscuit 1 inch apart on prepared baking sheet. Bake until golden brown, 10–15 minutes.

While biscuits are baking, melt 1 tablespoon of butter. When biscuits are done, remove from oven and brush tops with melted butter. Makes about 12 biscuits.

PUMPKIN QUICK BREAD

I can (15 ounces) or I $^{7}/_{8}$ cups	**cooked pumpkin puree**
2 cups	**sugar**
I cup	**vegetable oil**
$^{2}/_{3}$ cup	**water**
$^{1}/_{2}$ cup	**applesauce**
4	**eggs**
3 $^{1}/_{2}$ cups	**flour**
2 teaspoons	**baking soda**
I $^{1}/_{2}$ teaspoons	**salt**
I teaspoon	**cinnamon**
I teaspoon	**nutmeg**
$^{1}/_{2}$ teaspoon	**cloves**
$^{1}/_{2}$ teaspoon	**ginger**

Preheat oven to 350 degrees. Prepare three 3 x 7-inch loaf pans with nonstick cooking spray and dust with flour.

In a large bowl, mix together pumpkin, sugar, oil, water, applesauce, and eggs until well blended. In a separate bowl, whisk together the flour, baking soda, salt, cinnamon, nutmeg, cloves, and ginger. Stir flour mixture into pumpkin mixture just until blended. Divide evenly among the prepared pans.

Bake for about 50 minutes, or until loaves are lightly browned and a toothpick inserted in the center comes out clean. Cool on a wire rack for 10 minutes before removing from pan. Makes 3 loaves.

PUMPKIN STREUSEL COFFEE CAKE

1/2 cup plus 5 tablespoons	**butter or margarine,** softened, divided
1/2 cup plus 6 tablespoons	**packed dark brown sugar,** divided
1 1/2 cups	**canned or cooked pumpkin puree**
3	**eggs**
2 1/2 cups plus 6 tablespoons	**flour,** divided
2 teaspoons	**baking powder**
1/2 teaspoon	**salt**
1 tablespoon	**pumpkin pie spice**
6 tablespoons	**sugar**
1/2 teaspoon	**cinnamon**
1 1/4 cups	**powdered sugar**
1 teaspoon	**vanilla**
1–2 tablespoons	**maple syrup**

Preheat oven to 350 degrees and prepare a 9 x 9-inch baking dish with nonstick cooking spray.

In a medium bowl, combine 1/2 cup butter, 1/2 cup brown sugar, pumpkin, and eggs; beat until smooth. In a separate bowl, whisk together 2 1/2 cups flour, baking powder, salt, and pie spice. Add flour mixture to the pumpkin mixture; stir to combine. Pour into prepared dish. In a small saucepan, melt 5 tablespoons butter; transfer 3 tablespoons to a small bowl. To the bowl, add 6 tablespoons brown sugar, 6 tablespoons flour, sugar, and cinnamon. Mix until crumbly; sprinkle over cake batter. Bake for 45 minutes, or until a toothpick inserted in the center comes out clean. Cool for 10 minutes.

To the saucepan with 2 tablespoons melted butter, add the powdered sugar, vanilla, and 1 tablespoon syrup. Heat, stirring constantly, until mixture is smooth; add more syrup if needed. Drizzle glaze over cake. Makes 12 servings.

PUMPKIN MONKEY BREAD

1/2 cup	**sugar**
2 tablespoons	**pumpkin pie spice**
1/4 teaspoon	**salt**
4 tubes (7.5 ounces each)	**refrigerated buttermilk biscuits**
1 cup	**packed brown sugar**
1/2 cup	**butter or margarine**
1/2 cup	**canned or cooked pumpkin puree**
1/2 cup	**cream cheese,** softened

Preheat oven to 350 degrees and prepare a 6-cup fluted Bundt pan with nonstick cooking spray.

In a large bowl, combine the sugar, pie spice, and salt. Separate each can of dough into 10 biscuits, and cut each biscuit in quarters. Toss the biscuit pieces in the cinnamon sugar mixture and arrange in prepared pan.

In a saucepan over medium heat, combine the brown sugar, butter, pumpkin, and cream cheese, and stir with a whisk until butter is melted and mixture is smooth. Pour mixture evenly over biscuits and place the pan on a baking sheet in case it bubbles over.

Bake until golden brown, about 30–35 minutes. Remove from oven and cool in pan 2 minutes. Place heatproof serving plate over pan, turn over and gently lift off pan. Cool for 5 minutes before serving. Makes 8–10 servings.

SPICY PUMPKIN GINGERBREAD

3 cups	**sugar**
I cup	**vegetable oil**
4	**eggs**
$^2/_3$ cup	**water**
I can (15 ounces) or I $^7/_8$ cups	**cooked pumpkin puree**
2 teaspoons	**ginger**
I teaspoon	**allspice**
I teaspoon	**cinnamon**
I teaspoon	**cloves**
3 $^1/_2$ cups	**flour**
2 teaspoons	**baking soda**
I $^1/_2$ teaspoons	**salt**
$^1/_2$ teaspoon	**baking powder**
	whipped cream

Preheat oven to 325 degrees and prepare two 9 x 5-inch loaf pans with nonstick cooking spray.

In a large bowl, combine sugar, oil, eggs, and water; beat until well blended. Add pumpkin, ginger, allspice, cinnamon, and cloves; stir until smooth.

In a medium bowl, whisk together flour, baking soda, salt, and baking powder. Add the flour mixture to the pumpkin mixture and stir just until all ingredients are blended. Divide batter evenly between prepared pans. Bake until loaves are lightly browned and a toothpick inserted in the center comes out clean, about I hour and 15 minutes. Serve with whipped cream. Makes 2 loaves.

PUMPKIN CRISPIES

1 cup	**canned or cooked pumpkin puree**
8 ounces	**cream cheese,** softened
1/4 cup	**milk**
1/2 cup	**whipped topping**
1 package (3.4 ounces)	**instant vanilla pudding mix**
1/2 teaspoon	**pumpkin pie spice**
2/3 cup	**sugar**
1 teaspoon	**cinnamon**
2 tubes (16.3 ounces each)	**large refrigerated flaky biscuits**
	vegetable oil, for frying

In a small bowl, combine the pumpkin, cream cheese, milk, whipped topping, pudding mix, and pie spice; stir until smooth. Reserve.

In another small bowl, combine the sugar and cinnamon; reserve.

On a lightly floured surface, roll out each biscuit to a 6-inch diameter. Spread about 1/4 cup of the pumpkin mixture on half of each biscuit. Bring dough from opposite side over filling just until edges meet; pinch seams to seal.

In a deep-fat fryer, heat oil to 375 degrees. Fry crispies, a few at a time, until golden brown, about 1 minute. Turn and cook the other side until golden brown. Drain on paper towels and sprinkle generously on both sides with cinnamon sugar mixture. Makes 16 crispies.

PUMPKIN CHOCOLATE HAZELNUT ROLLS

1/2 cup	**canned or cooked pumpkin puree**
1/2 cup	**chocolate-hazelnut spread,** such as Nutella
2 packages (8 ounces each)	**seamless croissant dough sheets**
	powdered sugar

Preheat oven to 425 degrees and line two baking sheets with parchment paper.

In a small bowl, whisk together the pumpkin and the chocolate-hazelnut spread; reserve.

Unroll one dough sheet on a lightly floured work surface and flatten lightly with hands. Spread half of the pumpkin mixture evenly over the dough. Starting at the short end, roll the dough up and press the ends to seal. Repeat with remaining dough and filling. Put the rolls on one of the baking sheets and place in the freezer for 10 minutes to firm.

Remove from freezer and cut each roll into 8 slices. Arrange 8 slices on each prepared baking sheet. Bake until lightly browned, about 8–10 minutes. Cool on a wire rack for 10 minutes and sprinkle with powdered sugar. Makes 16 rolls.

PUMPKIN BEIGNETS

1/2 teaspoon	**dry yeast**
1/4 cup	**warm water**
4 cups	**flour**
1 cup	**canned or cooked pumpkin puree**
1/4 cup	**hot water**
1/4 cup	**sugar**
1/4 cup	**heavy cream**
1	**egg,** lightly beaten
2 tablespoons	**vegetable shortening**
1/2 teaspoon	**salt**
	vegetable oil, for frying
3 tablespoons	**butter or margarine**
1/4 cup	**maple syrup**
1 cup	**powdered sugar**

In a small bowl, sprinkle yeast over warm water and stir to dissolve; let stand for 5 minutes. In a large bowl, combine flour, pumpkin, hot water, sugar, cream, egg, shortening, salt, and yeast. Mix dough until combined and smooth. Cover bowl and let rest for 30 minutes. Transfer dough to a well-floured surface. Roll to a 1/4-inch thickness and cut into 2-inch squares. Cover and let dough rise until doubled, in a warm, draft-free area, about 1–1 1/2 hours.

Line a baking sheet with paper towels. Heat 3 inches of vegetable oil to 350 degrees in a deep fryer or a deep, heavy pot. Fry beignets until golden brown, about 2–3 minutes on each side. Drain on paper towels.

Combine butter and maple syrup in a small saucepan and heat until butter melts. Remove from heat and whisk in powdered sugar until smooth. Drizzle warm beignets with maple glaze and serve immediately. Makes 8 servings.

BREAKFASTS

PUMPKIN CHEESECAKE FRENCH TOAST

8	**¹/₂-inch thick slices French bread**
4 ounces	**cream cheese,** softened
¹/₂ cup	**canned or cooked pumpkin puree**
¹/₄ cup	**packed light brown sugar**
4 teaspoons	**vanilla,** divided
¹/₂ teaspoon	**pumpkin pie spice**
6 tablespoons	**butter or margarine,** divided
2	**eggs**
1 ¹/₂ cups	**milk**
¹/₄ cup	**sugar**
¹/₄ cup	**flour**
¹/₂ teaspoon	**salt**
2 tablespoons	**vegetable oil,** divided
	maple syrup

Preheat oven to 325 degrees. Arrange bread on a baking sheet and bake for 4 minutes on each side. Cool on a wire rack.

In a small bowl, combine cream cheese, pumpkin, brown sugar, 1 teaspoon vanilla, and pie spice. Spread half of the bread slices with the filling and top with remaining slices. In a small saucepan, melt 4 tablespoons of butter. Cool to room temperature and transfer to a shallow dish. Add the eggs, milk, 3 teaspoons vanilla, and sugar. Whisk in the flour and salt; reserve. Heat 1 tablespoon butter and 1 tablespoon oil in a large frying pan over medium-high heat. Dip 2 of the sandwiches in the egg mixture until bread is moistened. Cook until golden brown, about 2 minutes on each side. Wipe out frying pan and heat 1 tablespoon butter and 1 tablespoon oil. Cook remaining sandwiches as above. Serve with maple syrup. Makes 4 servings.

OVERNIGHT PUMPKIN BRULEE FRENCH TOAST

4 tablespoons	**butter or margarine,** melted
³/₄ cup	**packed dark brown sugar**
I teaspoon	**cinnamon**
6	**eggs,** slightly beaten
I ¹/₂ cups	**milk**
I cup	**canned or cooked pumpkin puree**
I tablespoon	**vanilla**
I ¹/₄ teaspoons	**pumpkin pie spice**
¹/₈ teaspoon	**salt**
I loaf	**French bread,** cut in I ¹/₂-inch thick slices
¹/₂ cup	**chopped pecans**
	powdered sugar
	maple syrup

Drizzle the melted butter in the bottom of a 9 x 13-inch baking dish, and sprinkle evenly with the brown sugar and cinnamon. Reserve. In a medium bowl, combine the eggs, milk, pumpkin, vanilla, pie spice, and salt; whisk until blended. Dip bread slices in the mixture and arrange in baking dish, overlapping if necessary. Pour any remaining pumpkin mixture evenly over the bread. Cover tightly with aluminum foil and refrigerate for at least 4 hours or overnight.

Preheat oven to 350 degrees.

When ready to bake, sprinkle pecans evenly over the top. Replace foil and bake for 30 minutes. Remove foil and continue baking until top is golden brown and a knife inserted in the center comes out clean, about 10–15 minutes. Remove from oven and cool for 5 minutes. Sprinkle with powdered sugar and serve with maple syrup. Makes 8 servings.

PUMPKIN PANCAKES

1 1/2 cups	**milk**
1 cup	**canned or cooked pumpkin puree**
1	**egg**
2 tablespoons	**vegetable oil**
2 tablespoons	**white vinegar**
2 cups	**flour**
3 tablespoons	**packed light brown sugar**
2 teaspoons	**pumpkin pie spice**
2 teaspoons	**baking powder**
1 teaspoon	**baking soda**
1/2 teaspoon	**salt**
	maple syrup

In a large bowl, mix together the milk, pumpkin, egg, oil, and vinegar. In a medium bowl, whisk together the flour, brown sugar, pie spice, baking powder, baking soda, and salt. Add the flour mixture to the pumpkin mixture and stir just until combined.

Heat a lightly greased griddle or frying pan over medium-high heat. Pour 1/4 cup batter on the griddle and spread out slightly using a spatula or spoon. Brown on both sides and serve hot with maple syrup. Makes about 12 pancakes.

PUMPKIN, ORANGE, AND CRANBERRY STRATA

7 cups	**1-inch bread cubes**
1 1/4 cups	**fresh or frozen, thawed whole cranberries**
3	**eggs**
2 1/2 cups	**milk**
I can (15 ounces) or 1 7/8 cups	**cooked pumpkin puree**
1/2 cup	**orange juice**
1 tablespoon	**grated orange peel**
2 teaspoons	**pumpkin pie spice**
1/2 cup	**packed brown sugar**
1 teaspoon	**vanilla**
3/4 teaspoon	**salt**
1 cup	**vanilla Greek yogurt**
1/2 cup	**maple syrup**

Prepare a 9 x 9-inch baking dish with nonstick cooking spray and spread half of the bread cubes evenly in the dish. Top with half of the cranberries; repeat layers and reserve.

In a large bowl, combine the eggs, milk, pumpkin, juice, peel, pie spice, brown sugar, vanilla, and salt; whisk until well blended. Pour over bread cubes and cover with aluminum foil. Refrigerate at least 4 hours or overnight.

Heat oven to 325 degrees. Leave the foil on the strata and bake for 30 minutes. Remove foil and continue baking until top is golden brown and a knife inserted in the center comes out clean, about 30–40 minutes. Remove from oven and cool for 5 minutes. Combine yogurt and maple syrup in a small bowl and serve over top of strata. Makes 9 servings.

PUMPKIN WAFFLES

3	**eggs,** separated
2 cups	**flour**
3 tablespoons	**packed dark brown sugar**
2 teaspoons	**baking powder**
1 teaspoon	**baking soda**
2 teaspoons	**pumpkin pie spice**
1/2 teaspoon	**salt**
1 1/2 cups	**milk**
1 can (15 ounces) or 1 7/8 cups	**cooked pumpkin puree**
4 tablespoons	**butter or margarine,** melted
2 tablespoons	**apple cider vinegar**
1 teaspoon	**vanilla**

Turn the oven to warm or lowest setting. In a large bowl, beat the egg whites with an electric mixer until stiff peaks form; reserve.

In a large bowl, whisk together the flour, brown sugar, baking powder, baking soda, pie spice, and salt. In a medium bowl, combine the milk, pumpkin, melted butter, 1 egg yolk (reserve others for another use), and vinegar; stir until blended. Add the pumpkin mixture to the flour mixture and stir to combine. Gently fold in egg whites.

Prepare a waffle iron with nonstick cooking spray and heat according to manufacturer's directions. Cook waffles until crispy. Transfer to a baking sheet and keep warm in the oven until ready to serve. Makes about 6 waffles.

PUMPKIN DUTCH BABY

1/3 cup	**walnuts,** toasted
1 cup	**flour**
1 tablespoon	**sugar**
1 1/2 teaspoons	**pumpkin pie spice**
1/8 teaspoon	**salt**
4	**eggs**
1 cup	**milk**
3/4 cup	**canned or cooked pumpkin puree**
1 teaspoon	**vanilla**
2 tablespoons	**butter or margarine**
7 tablespoons	**powdered sugar**
	maple syrup

Preheat oven to 350 degrees. Spread the walnuts on a baking sheet in a single layer and bake until fragrant and lightly toasted, about 8–10 minutes, stirring halfway through cooking time. Remove from oven and cool to room temperature; reserve.

Increase oven temperature to 425 degrees.

In a large bowl, whisk together the flour, sugar, pie spice, and salt. In a medium bowl, combine the eggs, milk, pumpkin, and vanilla; stir until blended. Add the pumpkin mixture to the flour mixture and beat with an electric mixer for 1 minute, until batter is smooth.

Add the butter to a 12-inch iron cast frying pan and put it in the oven. Cook until butter is melted, about 1–2 minutes. Remove pan from oven and carefully pour in batter. Return to oven and bake until golden brown, about 17–20 minutes. Remove from oven, dust with powdered sugar, and sprinkle with toasted walnuts. Serve warm with maple syrup. Makes 4 servings.

PUMPKIN PECAN MAPLE GRANOLA

2	**egg whites**
3/4 cup	**canned or cooked pumpkin puree**
1/2 cup	**maple syrup**
3 tablespoons	**packed dark brown sugar**
2 tablespoons	**butter or margarine,** melted
2 1/2 teaspoons	**pumpkin pie spice**
1 teaspoon	**vanilla**
1 pinch	**salt**
4 cups	**old-fashioned oats**
3/4 cup	**chopped pecans**
1/4 cup	**pepitas* (hulled green pumpkin seeds) or chopped almonds**
3/4 cup	**raisins**

Preheat oven to 325 degrees and line two large baking sheets with parchment paper or aluminum foil.

In a large bowl, whisk the egg whites until foamy. Add the pumpkin, maple syrup, brown sugar, butter, pie spice, vanilla, and salt; stir until well blended. Add the oats, pecans, and pepitas or almonds, and stir until combined.

Spread the mixture on the baking sheets, squeezing it together with your hands to form small clumps. Bake for 40–45 minutes, stirring once or twice, until golden. Remove from the oven and immediately stir in the raisins. Cool on baking sheets to room temperature. Store in an airtight container in the refrigerator for up to 2 weeks. Makes about 6 cups.

*Available in some supermarkets and specialty food stores.

CRISPY PUMPKIN CINNAMON ROLL-UPS

12 slices	**soft bread,** of choice
8 ounces	**cream cheese,** softened
1/2 cup	**canned or cooked pumpkin puree**
1	**egg yolk**
1/4 cup	**sugar**
1/2 teaspoon	**vanilla**
3/4 cup	**packed light brown sugar**
1/2 teaspoon	**cinnamon**
1/4 teaspoon	**salt**
1/2 cup	**butter or margarine,** melted

Line a baking sheet with parchment paper. Roll bread slices with a rolling pin to flatten slightly and trim off the crusts.

Beat the cream cheese, pumpkin, egg yolk, sugar, and vanilla in a medium bowl until combined. Divide the mixture among the bread slices and spread evenly. Roll up slices tightly jelly-roll style, pressing on the edges to seal.

Combine the brown sugar, cinnamon, and salt in a shallow bowl. Generously brush each roll on all sides with the melted butter and roll in the brown sugar mix. Arrange the roll-ups on parchment-lined baking sheet and freeze for 4 hours. Transfer to an airtight container or bag and keep frozen until ready to bake.

Preheat oven to 375 degrees.

Arrange the frozen roll-ups on a parchment-lined baking sheet. Bake for 20 minutes, or until hot and crispy. You can also make the roll-ups without freezing and bake them for 8–10 minutes at 375 degrees, or until browned and crispy. Makes 6 servings.

PUMPKIN PIE
BAKED OATMEAL

4 cups	**quick-cooking oats**
$^1/_2$ cup	**flour**
1 tablespoon	**baking powder**
2$^1/_2$ teaspoons	**pumpkin pie spice**
1 teaspoon	**salt**
2$^1/_4$ cups	**milk**
$^3/_4$ cup	**canned or cooked pumpkin puree**
$^1/_2$ cup	**applesauce**
$^1/_2$ cup	**vegetable oil**
$^1/_2$ cup	**packed dark brown sugar**
2	**eggs**
$^1/_4$ cup	**maple syrup**

Preheat oven to 350 degrees and prepare a 9 x 13-inch baking dish with nonstick cooking spray.

In a small bowl, whisk together the oats, flour, baking powder, pie spice, and salt; reserve.

In a stand mixer or large mixing bowl, beat together the milk, pumpkin, applesauce, oil, brown sugar, eggs, and maple syrup until smooth. Add the oat mixture and beat on low until combined. Pour the batter into prepared baking dish and bake until hot and bubbling, about 30–35 minutes. Cool for 5 minutes before serving. Makes 8 servings.

PUMPKIN, POTATO, AND BACON HASH

4 slices	**bacon,** diced
I	**medium onion,** diced (about I cup)
4	**large Yukon gold potatoes,** peeled and cut in $^{1}/_{2}$-inch dice (about 4 cups)
$^{1}/_{2}$ cup	**water**
I	**small baking pumpkin,** seeds removed, peeled and cut in $^{1}/_{2}$-inch dice (about 2 cups)
$^{1}/_{2}$ teaspoon	**salt**
$^{1}/_{2}$ teaspoon	**pepper**
4	**eggs**

In a large frying pan over medium-low heat, fry the bacon until crisp. Use a slotted spoon to transfer bacon to paper towels. Drain all but 2 tablespoons of drippings from the pan. Increase heat to medium and cook the onion, stirring frequently, until translucent, about 4 minutes. Add the potatoes and water; cover and cook over high heat until potatoes are soft, about 8 minutes. Remove lid and add pumpkin. Cook, stirring often to prevent sticking, until pumpkin is tender and potatoes are beginning to brown, 8–10 minutes. Add the bacon, sprinkle with salt and pepper and cook for 2 minutes.

Divide hash among 4 warm plates and return pan to the stove. Increase heat to medium-high and fry the eggs to desired doneness. Top each portion of hash with a fried egg. Makes 4 servings.

BAKED BABY PUMPKINS WITH EGGS AND SAUSAGE

4	**small baking pumpkins,** about 1 pound each
1/2 pound	**bulk breakfast sausage**
5	**eggs**
4 slices	**stale bread,** cut in 1/4-inch cubes
1 tablespoon	**chopped fresh Italian parsley**
1/2 teaspoon	**dried sage**
1/2 teaspoon	**salt**
1/2 teaspoon	**freshly ground pepper**
4 teaspoons	**grated Parmesan cheese,** divided

Preheat oven to 350 degrees and line a baking sheet with parchment paper or aluminum foil. Use a sharp knife to slice the top quarter off each pumpkin; remove the seeds and stringy pulp.

In a medium frying pan, cook the sausage until thoroughly cooked, 5–6 minutes. Remove from heat, drain grease, and cool to room temperature.

In a large bowl, whisk 1 egg until foamy and add the sausage, bread cubes, parsley, sage, salt, and pepper until well combined. Fill each pumpkin with the bread mixture to about 1 inch from the top, and transfer to prepared baking sheet. Bake until the pumpkins are fork tender, about 40–45 minutes. Remove pan from oven and use a spoon to gently flatten the stuffing in each pumpkin.

Increase oven temperature to 400 degrees. Crack 1 egg and gently pour over the stuffing mixture for each pumpkin, being careful not to break yolk; sprinkle each with 1 teaspoon cheese. Cover the pumpkins lightly with foil, return to oven, and bake until eggs are set to desired doneness, about 10–13 minutes. Makes 4 servings.

PUMPKIN CREPES
WITH BROWN SUGAR FILLING

2 cups	**milk**
2 tablespoons	**butter or margarine,** melted, plus extra for cooking
2	**eggs**
1/2 cup	**canned or cooked pumpkin puree**
1 teaspoon	**vanilla**
1 1/2 cups	**flour**
1 tablespoon	**sugar**
1 1/2 teaspoons	**pumpkin pie spice**
1/2 teaspoon	**baking powder**
1/2 teaspoon	**salt**
3/4 cup	**cream cheese,** softened
1/4 cup	**packed brown sugar**
1 tablespoon	**maple syrup**
	powdered sugar

In a large bowl, combine the milk, butter, eggs, pumpkin, and vanilla; whisk until smooth. In a medium bowl, whisk together the flour, sugar, pie spice, baking powder, and salt. Add to pumpkin mixture and whisk until smooth, adding more milk if necessary; mixture should be the consistency of heavy whipping cream. In a small bowl, combine the cream cheese, brown sugar, and maple syrup; reserve.

Brush a crepe pan or 8-inch nonstick frying pan with melted butter and heat over medium-high heat. Pour 1/3 cup batter into pan and swirl to coat bottom evenly. Cook until top appears dry, about 45 seconds. Turn and cook on second side, about 30 seconds. Repeat with remaining batter, wiping out pan and brushing with melted butter before cooking. Spread each crepe with some of the cream cheese filling, roll up, and sprinkle with powdered sugar. Makes about 10 crepes.

SOUPS AND STEWS

AUTUMN STEW IN A PUMPKIN

3 tablespoons	**vegetable oil,** divided
2 pounds	**beef chuck,** cut in 1-inch cubes
1 cup	**water**
3	**large potatoes,** peeled and cut in 1-inch cubes
4	**medium carrots,** peeled and cut in 1/4-inch slices
1	**large green bell pepper,** seeded and chopped
2 cloves	**garlic,** peeled and minced
1	**medium onion,** chopped
2 teaspoons	**salt**
1/2 teaspoon	**pepper**
2 tablespoons	**beef bouillon granules**
1 can (14 1/2 ounces)	**diced tomatoes,** with liquid
1	**large pumpkin (10–12 pounds)**

Heat 2 tablespoons of oil in a large pot, and brown the beef. Drain the grease and add the water, potatoes, carrots, bell pepper, garlic, onion, salt, and pepper. Cover and simmer for 2 hours. Stir in bouillon and tomatoes.

Preheat oven to 325 degrees and arrange rack on the bottom third.

Wash the pumpkin and cut a 6-inch circle around the top stem. Remove top, trim, and reserve. Scoop out the seeds and stringy pulp. Place pumpkin on a sturdy baking pan and carefully pour the stew inside. Replace the top and brush the outside with 1 tablespoon oil. Bake just until pumpkin is tender, 1 1/2–2 hours. Cool on the baking sheet for 5 minutes. Serve stew directly from the pumpkin, along with some of the cooked pumpkin. Makes 8–10 servings.

CREAMY PUMPKIN CARROT SOUP

2 tablespoons	**butter or margarine**
1	**medium onion,** diced
1 clove	**garlic,** peeled and minced
4 cups	**chicken broth**
3	**large carrots,** peeled and shredded
1 cup	**canned or cooked pumpkin puree**
1 cup	**half-and-half**
	salt and pepper, to taste
	chopped fresh parsley

In a heavy pot, melt the butter over medium heat and saute the onion and garlic until tender, stirring occasionally, about 5 minutes. Add the broth and carrots and simmer until the carrots are tender, about 15 minutes.

Working in batches, puree the soup in a blender or food processor until nearly smooth. Return to the pot and add the pumpkin and half-and-half. Stir and heat through, seasoning with salt and pepper. Garnish with chopped parsley. Makes 6 servings.

SLOW-COOKED PUMPKIN CHILI

2 pounds	**spicy bulk sausage**
1	**onion,** chopped
1	**red bell pepper,** chopped and diced
1	**green bell pepper,** chopped and diced
2 cans (15 ounces each)	**kidney beans,** drained and rinsed
1 can (26 ounces)	**tomato sauce**
1 can (15 ounces) or 1 7/8 cups	**cooked pumpkin puree**
1 cup	**chicken broth**
1 can (4 ounces)	**diced green chiles**
2 tablespoons	**chili powder**
1 1/2 teaspoons	**salt**
1/2 teaspoon	**pepper**
	sour cream
	grated cheese

In a large frying pan over medium heat, cook the sausage until browned; remove and drain on paper towels. Pour out all but 1 tablespoon of the drippings. Add the onion and peppers and saute over medium heat, stirring occasionally, until tender, 5–6 minutes.

Transfer the onion mixture to a 4-quart slow cooker and add the sausage, beans, tomato sauce, pumpkin, chicken broth, green chiles, chili powder, salt, and pepper. Cover and cook on low setting for 6–7 hours or high setting for 4–5 hours, adding water if mixture becomes too thick. Serve accompanied with sour cream and cheese. Makes 10–12 servings.

CURRIED PUMPKIN SOUP

2 tablespoons	**butter or margarine**
1/2 pound	**sliced fresh mushrooms**
1/2 cup	**chopped onion**
2 tablespoons	**flour**
1 teaspoon	**curry powder**
3 cups	**chicken broth**
1 can (15 ounces) or 1 7/8 cups	**cooked pumpkin puree**
1 1/2 cups	**half-and-half**
1/2 teaspoon	**salt**
1/4 teaspoon	**pepper**
	finely chopped fresh chives

In a large saucepan over medium heat, melt the butter and saute the mushrooms and onion until tender, about 5 minutes. Sprinkle the flour and curry powder into the onions and mushrooms and stir until blended. Gradually add the broth, stirring constantly to blend. Bring to a boil, reduce heat, and simmer, stirring constantly, until thickened, 2–3 minutes. Stir in the pumpkin, half-and-half, salt, and pepper, and cook until heated through. Garnish with chives. Makes 6 servings.

PUMPKIN AND BLACK BEAN SOUP

I tablespoon	**olive oil**
I	**onion,** diced
4 cloves	**garlic,** peeled and minced
6 cups	**chicken or vegetable broth**
2 cans (15 ounces each) or 3¾ cups	**cooked pumpkin puree**
2 cans (15 ounces each)	**black beans,** rinsed and drained
2	**bay leaves**
I teaspoon	**cumin**
I teaspoon	**salt**
¹/₂ teaspoon	**pepper**
¹/₂ teaspoon	**dried oregano**
I	**avocado,** peeled and cut in ¹/₂-inch cubes
	sour cream
2	**limes,** cut in wedges

Heat the oil in a large pot over medium heat and saute the onion until translucent, about 5 minutes. Add the garlic and saute for I minute. Add the broth, pumpkin, beans, bay leaves, cumin, salt, pepper, and oregano; stir until smooth. Cook, stirring often, until mixture comes to a boil. Reduce heat and simmer for 20 minutes. Remove bay leaves. Garnish with avocado and sour cream, and serve with lime wedges. Makes 8 servings.

COMFORTING PUMPKIN CHICKEN SOUP

4 tablespoons	**olive oil**
1 cup	**finely chopped onion**
1 cup	**diced celery**
1 cup	**diced carrots**
4 cloves	**garlic,** peeled and minced
3 cups	**cooked, shredded chicken**
4 cups	**chicken broth**
1 can (15 ounces) or 1$^7/_8$ cups	**cooked pumpkin puree**
$^1/_2$ cup	**heavy cream**
1 $^1/_2$ teaspoons	**salt**
$^1/_2$ teaspoon	**pepper**
1 cup	**grated cheddar cheese**
$^1/_4$ cup	**finely chopped fresh cilantro**

Heat oil in a large pot over medium heat. Add the onion, celery, and carrots, and saute, stirring frequently, until tender, 10–12 minutes. Add the garlic and continue cooking for 1 minute. Add the chicken, broth, pumpkin, cream, salt, and pepper. Cook, stirring often, until soup is heated through. Add the cheese and stir just until melted. Remove from heat and serve garnished with cilantro. Makes 8 servings.

PUMPKIN POTATO SOUP

3 tablespoons	**olive oil,** divided
1	**medium onion,** chopped
2 cloves	**garlic,** peeled and minced
2	**medium potatoes,** peeled and diced
1/2 teaspoon	**chili powder**
1/2 teaspoon	**cumin**
6 cups	**chicken or vegetable broth**
1 cup	**canned or cooked pumpkin puree**
1/4 cup	**half-and-half,** heated
	salt and pepper
	chopped fresh parsley

Heat 2 tablespoons of oil in a large pot over medium heat. Add the onion, garlic, potatoes, chili powder, and cumin; saute for 5 minutes. Add the broth and continue cooking, stirring occasionally, until the potatoes are tender, about 15 minutes.

Process half of the soup in a blender or food processor until smooth; return to the pot. Add the pumpkin and half-and-half, and cook, stirring frequently, until mixture is hot. Season to taste with salt and pepper, and serve garnished with parsley. Makes 6 servings.

PUMPKIN, CORN, AND SHRIMP BISQUE

1 tablespoon	**olive oil**
1	**medium onion,** chopped
2 cloves	**garlic,** peeled and minced
1	**green bell pepper,** chopped
2 cans (15 ounces each) or 3¾ cups	**cooked pumpkin puree**
4 cups	**chicken or vegetable broth**
1½ teaspoons	**seafood seasoning,** such as Old Bay
¼ teaspoon	**pepper**
2 cans (14½ ounces each)	**cream-style corn**
1½ pounds	**medium shrimp,** peeled and deveined
	finely chopped green onions

In a large pot over medium heat, heat the oil and saute the onion, garlic, and bell pepper until tender, 6–7 minutes. Add the pumpkin, broth, seafood seasoning, pepper, and corn. Stir to combine and heat, stirring frequently, until mixture simmers. Reduce heat to low and cook, stirring often, for 15 minutes. Add shrimp, increase heat to medium and cook until shrimp are pink and opaque, 4–7 minutes. Serve garnished with green onions. Makes 8 servings.

PUMPKIN TORTILLA SOUP

1	**cooked rotisserie chicken,** about 2 pounds
1 tablespoon	**olive oil**
1	**large onion,** chopped
1	**leek,** white and pale green parts only, cleaned and sliced
6 cups	**chicken broth**
2 cans (10 ounces each)	**diced tomatoes and green chiles,** with liquid
2 cups	**vegetable juice like V-8 or tomato juice**
1 can (15 ounces) or 1 $7/8$ cups	**cooked pumpkin puree**
2 stalks	**celery,** chopped
2 cloves	**garlic,** peeled and minced
$1/2$ teaspoon	**salt**
$1/2$ teaspoon	**pepper**
1 bag (13 ounces)	**tortilla chips**
$1/4$ cup	**fresh cilantro leaves**
8 ounces	**grated Monterey Jack cheese**

Remove the chicken meat from the bones and cut or tear into medium-size pieces; reserve.

Heat the oil in a large pot over medium heat and saute the onions and leeks until tender, 6–7 minutes. Add the broth, tomatoes and chiles, juice, pumpkin, celery, garlic, salt, and pepper and stir to combine. Increase heat and cook until almost boiling; reduce heat to medium-low and simmer for 1 hour. Add the chicken and simmer for 15 more minutes.

Divide the tortilla chips among 8 soup bowls and gently crush. Ladle the soup over the chips and garnish with cilantro and cheese. Makes 8 servings.

SIDE DISHES

PUMPKIN FRIES
WITH HONEY MUSTARD

1/2 cup	**mayonnaise**
1 tablespoon	**yellow mustard**
1 1/2 tablespoons	**honey**
1 pinch	**cayenne pepper**
1	**small baking pumpkin,** about 1 pound
2 tablespoons	**olive oil**
1 1/2 teaspoons	**pumpkin pie spice**
2 teaspoons	**cinnamon**
1 teaspoon	**salt**

Preheat oven to 350 degrees and line a baking sheet with parchment paper.

In a small bowl, combine the mayonnaise, mustard, honey, and pepper; stir until smooth. Cover and refrigerate.

Halve the pumpkin and remove the stem, seeds, and pulp; use a vegetable peeler to remove the skin. Use a sharp knife to cut pumpkin into 1/4–1/2-inch strips, 3–4 inches long. Transfer to a medium bowl and drizzle with the olive oil. Sprinkle with the pie spice, cinnamon, and salt; stir to coat.

Spread the fries in a single layer on prepared baking sheet. Cook until lightly browned and just tender, stirring occasionally, about 30–35 minutes. Drain on paper towels and serve with honey mustard. Makes about 4 servings.

PUMPKIN MASHED POTATOES

8	**medium russet potatoes,** peeled and quartered
I can (15 ounces) or 1 $\frac{7}{8}$ cups	**cooked pumpkin puree**
8 ounces	**cream cheese,** softened
$\frac{1}{2}$ cup	**cream**
$\frac{1}{2}$ cup	**butter or margarine,** softened
I teaspoon	**garlic powder**
I teaspoon	**salt**
$\frac{1}{4}$ teaspoon	**paprika**

Preheat oven to 350 degrees and prepare a 9 x 13-inch baking dish with nonstick cooking spray.

Fill a large pot with water and heat to boiling over medium-high heat. Cook the potatoes until tender, about 15–20 minutes. Drain in a strainer, return to the pot, and mash with a potato masher until almost smooth.

Add the pumpkin, cream cheese, cream, butter, garlic powder, and salt, and mash together until well combined. Spread in the prepared baking dish and sprinkle with paprika. Bake until top is lightly browned, about 30 minutes. Makes 10 servings.

ROASTED PUMPKIN AND ACORN SQUASH

1	**small baking pumpkin,** about 1 pound
1	**large acorn squash,** about 1 pound
2	**medium sweet onions,** quartered
1/4 cup	**olive oil**
	salt and pepper
	chopped fresh parsley

Preheat oven to 400 degrees.

Peel the skin from the pumpkin and squash. Cut in half and remove the seeds and stem. Cut in 1-inch cubes. Transfer to a large bowl and add the onions. Drizzle with olive oil and stir to coat.

Spread the mixture evenly in a large roasting pan and season with salt and pepper. Roast until the pumpkin and squash are lightly browned and just tender, stirring occasionally, 45–60 minutes. Garnish with parsley before serving. Makes 8 servings.

PUMPKIN SPOON BREAD

3	**eggs,** separated
2 1/2 cups	**milk**
1/2 cup	**butter or margarine**
1 1/2 teaspoons	**salt**
1 cup	**stone-ground yellow cornmeal**
1 cup	**canned or cooked pumpkin puree**
2	**green onions,** finely chopped
1/4 teaspoon	**pepper**

Preheat oven to 350 degrees and prepare a 9 x 4-inch loaf pan with nonstick cooking spray.

In a medium bowl, beat the egg whites using an electric mixer until soft peaks form; reserve.

In a large saucepan over medium heat, combine the milk, butter, and salt, and cook, stirring frequently, until mixture comes to a simmer. Reduce heat and gradually whisk in the cornmeal. Simmer while stirring until thickened, about 2 minutes. Remove from heat and add the pumpkin, stirring to blend. Cool for 10 minutes and reserve.

In a large bowl, whisk together the egg yolks, green onions, and pepper. Add the cooled cornmeal mixture and stir to blend. Whisk 1/4 of the egg whites into the cornmeal mixture. Gently fold in the remaining egg whites. Pour the batter in the prepared pan and bake for 40–45 minutes, or until bread starts to pull away from the pan. Serve warm. Makes 6 servings.

CRISPY PUMPKIN POTATO BAKE

2 tablespoons	**butter or margarine**
2	**large onions,** thinly sliced
1 cup	**half-and-half**
1 cup	**canned or cooked pumpkin puree**
1 teaspoon	**salt**
1/2 teaspoon	**pepper**
3 pounds	**Yukon Jack potatoes,** peeled and cut in 1/4-inch slices
2 cups	**soft breadcrumbs**
8 ounces	**grated Gruyere or Swiss cheese**

Preheat oven to 350 degrees and prepare a 9 x 13-inch baking pan with nonstick cooking spray.

Melt the butter in a large frying pan over medium heat and cook the onions, stirring frequently, for 15 minutes or until golden brown.

In a medium bowl, whisk together the half-and-half, pumpkin, salt, and pepper. Arrange the onions and potatoes in alternating layers in the prepared pan and pour the pumpkin mixture evenly over the top. Cover with aluminum foil and bake for 75 minutes.

Remove from the oven and increase the oven temperature to 400 degrees. Sprinkle the breadcrumbs and cheese evenly on top of the mixture and bake, uncovered, for 15–20 minutes, or until golden brown. Makes 12 servings.

MAPLE ROASTED PUMPKIN AND BRUSSELS SPROUTS

1/2 cup	**chopped pecans**
1	**small baking pumpkin,** about 1 pound, peeled and cubed
2 tablespoons	**olive oil**
2 tablespoons	**maple syrup**
1 pound	**Brussels sprouts,** halved lengthwise **salt and pepper**

Preheat oven to 400 degrees. Spread the pecans on a baking sheet and bake, stirring once, until lightly toasted, about 5 minutes; reserve and wipe off the baking sheet.

In a medium bowl, combine the pumpkin, oil, and syrup; stir. Spread on a baking sheet and bake for 20 minutes, stirring once midway through cooking time.

Remove from oven, add the Brussels sprouts, and stir to combine. Return to oven and bake until pumpkin and sprouts are tender, about 20 minutes, stirring once midway through cooking time. Remove from oven and season to taste with salt and pepper. Sprinkle with chopped pecans. Makes 6 servings.

PUMPKIN FRITTERS

1 cup	**canned or cooked pumpkin puree**
1	**egg,** lightly beaten
1 cup	**flour**
1 teaspoon	**baking powder**
1 teaspoon	**curry powder**
1 teaspoon	**salt,** plus extra for sprinkling
	vegetable oil for frying

In a medium bowl, combine the pumpkin and egg and stir until blended.

In a small bowl, whisk together the flour, baking powder, curry powder, and salt until combined. Add the flour mixture to the pumpkin mixture and stir just until blended.

Fill a deep fryer or deep, heavy-bottomed saucepan with 2 inches of vegetable oil and heat to 325 degrees. Carefully drop batter by spoonfuls into hot oil and fry until golden brown, about 2 minutes, turning halfway through cooking time. Remove with a slotted spoon to paper towels to drain, sprinkle lightly with salt, and serve immediately. Makes about 24 fritters.

CAULIFLOWER PUMPKIN GRATIN

1	**medium cauliflower,** about 3 pounds, cut in 2-inch pieces
4 tablespoons	**butter or margarine,** divided
3 tablespoons	**flour**
2 cups	**hot milk**
1/2 cup	**canned or cooked pumpkin puree**
1 teaspoon	**salt**
1/2 teaspoon	**pepper**
1/4 teaspoon	**nutmeg**
3/4 cup	**grated Swiss cheese,** divided
1/2 cup	**grated Parmesan cheese**
1/2 cup	**fresh whole wheat breadcrumbs**

Preheat oven to 375 degrees and prepare a 9 x 13-inch baking dish with nonstick cooking spray. Bring a large pot of water to boil and cook the cauliflower until tender but still firm, 5–6 minutes. Drain.

Melt 2 tablespoons butter in a medium saucepan over low heat. Add the flour, and whisk constantly for 2 minutes. Add the hot milk and cook, whisking constantly, until mixture comes to a boil and thickens. Whisk in the pumpkin and remove from heat. Add the salt, pepper, nutmeg, 1/2 cup Swiss cheese, and Parmesan cheese; stir just until blended. Pour 1/3 of the sauce on the bottom of the baking dish. Arrange the cauliflower on top and pour the rest of the sauce evenly over top. Combine the breadcrumbs with remaining 1/4 cup Swiss cheese in a small bowl and sprinkle on top. Melt the remaining 2 tablespoons butter in a small saucepan, and drizzle over the gratin. Sprinkle with salt and pepper. Bake until bubbly and top is browned, about 30–35 minutes. Makes 8 servings.

DINNERS

GLAZED
PUMPKIN BBQ MEATLOAF

2 pounds	**ground beef**
1/2 cup	**seasoned breadcrumbs**
1 cup	**canned or cooked pumpkin puree,** divided
1	**egg**
1/2 teaspoon	**garlic powder**
1 teaspoon	**chili powder,** divided
3/4 teaspoon	**salt,** divided
1/2 teaspoon	**pepper,** divided
1 cup	**ketchup**
1 clove	**garlic,** peeled and minced
1 tablespoon	**water**
1 tablespoon	**apple cider vinegar**
1 tablespoon	**dark brown sugar**

Preheat oven to 400 degrees and prepare a rimmed baking sheet with nonstick cooking spray.

In a large bowl, combine the ground beef, breadcrumbs, 1/2 cup pumpkin, egg, garlic powder, 1/2 teaspoon chili powder, 1/2 teaspoon salt, and 1/4 teaspoon pepper. Thoroughly mix ingredients together and form in a loaf shape about 9 x 5 inches. Transfer to the baking sheet and bake for about 1 hour, or until thermometer registers 160 degrees when inserted in the center of the loaf. Cool in pan for 10 minutes before slicing.

Combine the ketchup, 1/2 cup pumpkin, garlic, water, vinegar, brown sugar, and 1/2 teaspoon chili powder, 1/4 teaspoon salt, and 1/4 teaspoon pepper in a small saucepan. Cook over medium heat, stirring until sauce is thick. Cut meatloaf in 1-inch slices and drizzle with the sauce. Makes 6 servings.

PUMPKIN RAVIOLI

1 cup	**canned or cooked pumpkin puree**
1/3 cup	**grated Parmesan cheese,** plus extra for garnish
1 1/4 teaspoons	**salt,** divided
1/8 teaspoon	**pepper**
24	**wonton wrappers**
1 1/2 tablespoons	**butter**
1/2 cup	**chicken broth**
	chopped flat-leaf parsley

Combine pumpkin, cheese, 1/4 teaspoon salt, and pepper in a small bowl and stir to blend. Spoon 2 teaspoons of the mixture in the center of each wonton wrapper. Moisten the edges of each wrapper with water and bring edges together diagonally to form a triangle; pinch edges to seal.

Bring a large pot of water and the remaining 1 teaspoon salt to a boil. Add the ravioli to the water and cook for 5–7 minutes, or until tender. While the ravioli is cooking, melt the butter in a large saucepan and add the chicken broth. Heat until the mixture simmers; keep warm. Drain the ravioli in a colander and add it to the broth mixture, stirring gently to coat. Garnish with parsley and additional cheese. Makes 4 servings.

PUMPKIN BACON BROCCOLI PASTA

1 tablespoon	**butter or margarine**
1	**medium onion,** thinly sliced
1 can (15 ounces) or 1⅞ cups	**cooked pumpkin puree**
1 cup	**chicken broth**
1 cup	**half-and-half**
2 tablespoons	**olive oil**
1 clove	**garlic,** peeled and minced
1 teaspoon	**salt**
½ teaspoon	**dried sage**
¼ teaspoon	**pepper**
1 pound	**uncooked bow tie pasta**
1 pound	**broccoli stems and florets,** chopped
6 slices	**bacon,** cooked, drained, and crumbled
1 cup	**grated mozzarella cheese**
¼ cup	**grated Parmesan cheese**
	chopped flat-leaf parsley

Heat the butter in a large frying pan and cook the onions until they are caramelized, about 20–30 minutes; reserve. In a blender or food processor, puree the pumpkin, broth, half-and-half, oil, garlic, salt, sage, and pepper until smooth. Add mixture to the onions and cook over medium heat for 5 minutes, stirring constantly; reserve.

Preheat oven to 350 degrees and prepare a 9 x 13-inch baking dish with nonstick cooking spray. In a large pot, cook the pasta al dente according to package directions, adding the broccoli the last 3 minutes of cooking. Drain water and return pasta and broccoli to the pot. Add the pumpkin mixture, bacon, and ½ cup mozzarella cheese; stir until combined. Transfer to prepared dish and sprinkle with remaining cheeses; cover with foil and bake until bubbly, about 20 minutes. Garnish with parsley. Makes 8 servings.

PUMPKIN APPLE PECAN CHICKEN

3/4 cup	**chopped pecans,** divided
1/2 cup	**canned or cooked pumpkin puree**
1/4 cup	**Italian seasoned breadcrumbs**
1/4 cup	**chopped dried apples**
1/2 teaspoon	**salt**
1/4 teaspoon	**pepper**
4	**boneless chicken breast halves,** pounded to a 1/2-inch thickness
2/3 cup	**prepared apple butter**
1/2 cup	**Italian salad dressing**

Preheat oven to 350 degrees and prepare an 8 x 8-inch baking dish with nonstick cooking spray.

Spread the pecans evenly on a baking sheet and bake until fragrant and lightly toasted, about 5 minutes. Remove from oven and reserve.

In a small bowl, combine the pumpkin, breadcrumbs, apples, 1/4 cup pecans, salt, and pepper. Spoon 1/4 of the mixture in the center of each chicken breast half. Wrap chicken around mixture and fasten with wooden toothpicks. Arrange chicken in prepared baking dish, seam side down.

In a small dish, combine the apple butter and Italian dressing and stir until smooth. Pour mixture evenly over chicken. Bake, basting frequently, for about 50 minutes, or until an instant-read thermometer registers 165 degrees when inserted in the center of the chicken. Garnish with remaining 1/2 cup pecans. Makes 4 servings.

AUTUMN LASAGNA

I pound	**bulk Italian sausage**
2 teaspoons	**olive oil**
I	**small onion,** chopped
1/2 pound	**sliced fresh mushrooms**
3/4 teaspoon	**salt,** divided
1/4 teaspoon	**pepper**
I can (15 ounces) or 1⅞ cups	**cooked pumpkin puree**
1/2 cup	**milk**
I cup	**ricotta cheese,** divided
2 teaspoons	**chopped fresh basil**
12	**no-cook lasagna noodles**
I cup	**grated mozzarella cheese,** divided
3/4 cup	**grated Parmesan cheese,** divided

Preheat oven to 375 degrees and prepare a 9 x 13-inch baking dish with nonstick cooking spray.

In a large frying pan, brown the sausage until cooked; remove and drain on paper towels. Clean the pan. Add the olive oil and saute the onion, about 3 minutes. Add the mushrooms and cook until mushrooms and onions are lightly browned, about 4 minutes. Sprinkle with 1/4 teaspoon salt and pepper. Remove from heat, cover and reserve. In a medium bowl, combine the pumpkin, milk, and 1/4 teaspoon salt. In a small bowl, combine the ricotta, basil, and 1/4 teaspoon salt. Spread 1/2 cup of pumpkin mixture in prepared dish and top with 4 noodles. Add 1/2 cup pumpkin sauce over noodles, spreading to edges. Top with half of the sausage mixture, 1/2 cup ricotta, 1/2 cup mozzarella and 1/4 cup Parmesan cheese. Repeat layers. Top with remaining noodles and sauce. Cover and bake for 45 minutes. Uncover and top with 1/4 cup Parmesan cheese. Continue baking until bubbling and cheese is melted, about 10–15 minutes. Let stand for 10 minutes before cutting. Makes 6 servings.

PUMPKIN RISOTTO

1	**small sugar pumpkin,** seeds removed, peeled and cut in $1/2$-inch dice (about $1 1/2$ cups)
2 tablespoons	**butter**
2 tablespoons	**olive oil**
1	**large onion,** chopped
3 cloves	**garlic,** peeled and minced
$1 1/2$ cups	**Arborio rice**
$1/2$ pound	**button mushrooms,** cleaned and sliced
7–8 cups	**hot chicken broth or stock**
$2/3$ cup	**grated Parmesan cheese**
	salt and pepper
$1/2$ cup	**chopped flat-leaf parsley**

In a large frying pan over medium heat, melt the butter and oil together and saute the onion until translucent, about 5 minutes. Add the garlic and cook for 1 more minute. Add the rice and cook, stirring, for 1 minute. Add the pumpkin, mushrooms, and 1 cup of hot broth. Cook, stirring often, until the liquid is almost absorbed. Continue stirring and adding broth $3/4$ cup at a time until the rice is tender, about 20 minutes. Sprinkle with the cheese and stir just until melted. Garnish with parsley. Makes 6 servings.

PUMPKIN TURKEY ENCHILADAS

1/2 cup	**vegetable oil**
18	**6-inch corn tortillas**
3/4 cup	**finely chopped onion**
3/4 cup	**canned or cooked pumpkin puree,** divided
3 cups	**chopped cooked turkey**
2 cups	**grated Monterey Jack cheese,** divided
1/4 cup	**butter or margarine**
1/4 cup	**flour**
2 cups	**chicken broth**
1 can (4 ounces)	**chopped green chiles**
3/4 cup	**sour cream**
	chopped green onions

Preheat oven to 375 degrees and prepare a 9 x 13-inch baking dish with nonstick cooking spray.

Heat oil in a medium frying pan until it shimmers. Cook each tortilla just until softened, about 10 seconds; drain on paper towels. Pour out the oil but do not wipe out pan. Return to heat and saute the onion, until translucent, about 5 minutes. Add 1/4 cup pumpkin and cook until heated through. Transfer mixture to a large bowl and add the turkey and 1 1/2 cups cheese; stir until combined. Divide mixture evenly in the center of each tortilla. Roll tortillas around the filling and arrange seam side down in prepared baking dish. In a large saucepan, melt the butter. Add the flour and whisk to combine. Whisk in the broth, stirring constantly, until mixture thickens. Stir in the chiles, 1/2 cup pumpkin, and sour cream until heated, pour evenly over enchiladas. Cover with foil and bake until hot, about 20–25 minutes. Top with 1/2 cup cheese and return to oven for 5 more minutes. Serve garnished with green onions. Makes 6–8 servings.

HEARTY PUMPKIN SHEPHERD'S PIE

1 pound	**russet potatoes,** peeled and quartered
6 tablespoons	**butter or margarine**
¾ cup	**milk**
1 cup	**canned or cooked pumpkin puree**
	salt and pepper, to taste
1 pound	**ground beef**
¼ cup	**water**
1	**medium onion,** chopped
2	**large carrots,** peeled and chopped
1 tablespoon	**flour**
1 tablespoon	**tomato paste**
1 tablespoon	**Worcestershire Sauce**
1 cup	**beef broth or stock**
1 can (15 ounces)	**corn,** drained
1½ cups	**grated sharp cheddar cheese**

Preheat oven to 425 degrees and prepare a 2-quart baking dish with nonstick cooking spray.

Add the potatoes to a large pot of boiling water and cook until tender, about 15–20 minutes. Drain water and mash the potatoes and butter until melted. Add the milk and pumpkin and mash until smooth. Season with salt and pepper. In a large frying pan, cook and crumble the ground beef. Transfer to a plate and reserve. Drain excess grease from pan and add water. Add the onion and carrots and cook about 6 minutes. Stir in the flour until blended. Add tomato paste and Worcestershire sauce. Add broth, corn, and cooked beef, and continue cooking until mixture thickens, about 10 minutes. Season with salt and pepper and transfer to prepared dish; sprinkle with cheese. Spoon potato mixture over top of cheese and bake until bubbly and lightly browned, 20–25 minutes. Makes 6–8 servings.

ROAST PUMPKIN, SAUSAGE, AND CARAMELIZED ONION PIZZA

1	**small baking pumpkin,** about 1 pound
2 tablespoons	**butter or margarine**
$1/2$ cup	**sliced onion**
1 pound	**prepared pizza dough**
$3/4$ pound	**bulk Italian sausage**
$1/2$–$2/3$ cup	**pizza sauce**
$1 1/2$ cups	**grated mozzarella cheese**

Wash the pumpkin, cut out the top and stem, and scoop out the seeds and stringy pulp. Cut the pumpkin in half and peel the skin. Cut into $1/2$-inch cubes to measure 1 cup; reserve. You may have some left over.

Heat the butter in a large frying pan over low heat, add the pumpkin and onion, and cook, stirring occasionally, until pumpkin is tender and onions are deep golden brown, about 20–30 minutes; reserve.

Preheat oven to 400 degrees.

Flatten the dough out on an ungreased 14-inch pizza pan and prick thoroughly with a fork. Bake until lightly browned, about 10–12 minutes. While dough is cooking, cook the sausage in a large frying pan over medium heat until no longer pink; drain. Spread a thin layer of the pizza sauce over the crust and top with the pumpkin-onion mixture. Top with the sausage and sprinkle with cheese. Bake until golden brown, about 10–12 minutes. Cut in wedges to serve. Makes 6 servings.

CREAMY PUMPKIN MAC AND CHEESE

I pound	**uncooked elbow macaroni**
1/4 cup	**butter or margarine**
1/4 cup	**flour**
2 cups	**milk**
1/2 teaspoon	**salt**
1/4 teaspoon	**pepper**
I teaspoon	**Dijon mustard**
I cup	**canned or cooked pumpkin puree**
2 1/2 cups	**grated cheddar cheese,** divided

In a large pot of salted boiling water, cook macaroni as directed on package.

While macaroni is cooking, melt butter in a medium saucepan over low heat. Add flour and whisk for I minute. Remove from heat and stir in milk. Return to heat and continue cooking until mixture thickens and starts to simmer. Add the salt, pepper, mustard, and pumpkin, and stir until combined. Add 2 cups of cheese, and stir until the cheese has melted.

When macaroni is done, drain and add to the cheese sauce, stirring to coat; adjust seasonings, if needed. Sprinkle the remaining cheese over top and serve. Makes 6 servings.

DESSERTS

PERFECT PUMPKIN PIE

1 (9-inch)	**unbaked pie crust**
1 can (15 ounces) or 1 7/8 cups	**cooked pumpkin puree**
1 can (14 ounces)	**sweetened condensed milk**
2	**eggs**
1 teaspoon	**cinnamon**
1/2 teaspoon	**ginger**
1/2 teaspoon	**nutmeg**
1/2 teaspoon	**salt**
	whipped cream

Preheat oven to 425 degrees.

Fit the pie crust into a 9-inch pie pan and crimp the edges. Fit a piece of aluminum foil inside the shell and fill with pie weights or dried beans. Bake the pie shell for 10 minutes, remove the foil and pie weights, and bake for 5 more minutes; cool on a wire rack to room temperature.

In a medium bowl, whisk together the pumpkin, condensed milk, eggs, cinnamon, ginger, nutmeg, and salt until smooth. Pour into crust. Bake 15 minutes.

Reduce oven temperature to 350 degrees and continue baking 35–40 minutes, or until a knife inserted in the center comes out clean. Remove from oven and let cool on a wire rack to room temperature. Serve with whipped cream. Makes 8 servings.

DEEP DISH
PUMPKIN CUSTARD PIE

1 (9-inch)	**unbaked pie crust**
1 package (8 ounces)	**cream cheese,** softened
2 cups	**canned or cooked pumpkin puree**
1 cup	**sugar**
$1/4$ teaspoon	**salt**
2	**eggs,** lightly beaten
$1/2$ cup	**half-and-half**
$1/4$ cup	**butter or margarine,** melted
1 teaspoon	**vanilla**
1 $1/4$ teaspoons	**pumpkin pie spice**
	whipped cream

Fit the pie crust into a 9-inch, deep dish pie pan and press along the bottom and up the sides; crimp edges. Freeze the pie shell for 1 hour.

Preheat oven to 375 degrees. Fit a piece of aluminum foil inside the shell and fill with pie weights or dried beans. Bake for 10 minutes, remove the foil and pie weights, and bake for 5 more minutes; cool on a wire rack to room temperature.

In a large bowl, beat the cream cheese and pumpkin with an electric mixer until combined. Add the sugar and salt, and beat until combined. Add the eggs, half-and-half, and melted butter, and beat until combined. Add the vanilla and pie spice, and beat until incorporated.

Pour the filling into the cooled pie crust and bake for about 50 minutes (cover crust edge with foil if it begins to overbrown), or until the center is nearly set. Remove from oven and let cool on a wire rack to room temperature. Serve topped with whipped cream. Makes 8 servings.

PUMPKIN CHIFFON PIE

1 cup	**chopped walnuts**
1 cup	**graham cracker crumbs**
1/4 cup	**packed dark brown sugar**
5 tablespoons	**butter or margarine,** melted
1/4 cup	**milk**
2 teaspoons	**vanilla**
1 packet (1/4 ounce)	**granulated unsweetened gelatin**
2/3 cup	**packed light brown sugar**
4	**eggs**
1 cup	**canned or cooked pumpkin puree**
2 teaspoons	**pumpkin pie spice**
1/8 teaspoon	**salt**
1 1/2 cups	**heavy cream**

Preheat oven to 350 degrees.

In a food processor or blender, pulse walnuts until finely ground. Add graham cracker crumbs and dark brown sugar and pulse. Drizzle in melted butter and pulse to blend. Press mixture into a 9-inch pie plate and bake until lightly browned, 10–15 minutes. Cool and reserve.

In a large saucepan, whisk together the milk, vanilla, and gelatin over low heat, stirring constantly until gelatin is completely dissolved, 2–3 minutes. Whisk in light brown sugar and stir until combined. Add the eggs, one at a time; whisking constantly. Add the pumpkin, pie spice, and salt, and continue whisking over low heat until custard is thick and smooth. Do not allow to boil. Pour custard in a large glass or ceramic bowl, cover and cool to room temperature.

In a medium bowl, whip cream to stiff peaks. Fold cream into cooled custard. Spoon in cooled pie shell, and refrigerate for at least 2 hours before serving. Makes 8 servings.

PUMPKIN CREAM PIE

1 box (3 ounces)	**cook and serve vanilla pudding**
1 cup	**half-and-half**
1 cup	**heavy cream,** divided
1/2 teaspoon	**pumpkin pie spice**
2/3 cup	**canned or cooked pumpkin puree**
2 tablespoons	**packed brown sugar**
1 (9-inch)	**prepared graham cracker pie crust**
1	**cinnamon graham cracker,** finely crushed

In a medium saucepan, combine pudding, half-and-half, 1/2 cup cream, and pie spice. Bring to a boil over medium heat, stirring constantly, until mixture is bubbly and thick. Remove from heat, add pumpkin, and stir to combine. Cover and cool to room temperature. Refrigerate for 2 hours.

In a large bowl, combine the remaining 1/2 cup cream and brown sugar. Beat until light and fluffy. Fold in pumpkin cream mixture until combined, and pour into the crust. Cover and refrigerate for 2 hours or overnight. Top with crushed graham cracker crumbs. Makes 8 servings.

NO-BAKE PUMPKIN CARAMEL CREAM PIE

I can (15 ounces) or 1⅞ cups	**cooked pumpkin puree**
I can (12 ounces)	**evaporated milk,** chilled
I box (3.4 ounces)	**instant vanilla pudding mix**
I teaspoon	**pumpkin pie spice,** plus extra for garnish
I tub (8 ounces)	**frozen whipped topping,** thawed, divided
I can (13.4 ounces)	**dulce de leche***
I (9-inch)	**prepared graham cracker pie crust**

In a large bowl, combine the pumpkin, evaporated milk, pudding mix, and pie spice; beat with an electric mixer until well blended, about 1 minute. Gently fold in 2 cups of the whipped topping.

Warm the dulce de leche in a microwave-safe bowl on high power for 15–20 seconds, just until mixture can be stirred; stir well. Drizzle the caramel evenly over the crust. Pour in the pumpkin filling and smooth top with a spatula. Refrigerate for at least 3 hours or overnight. Garnish with remaining whipped topping and a sprinkle of pumpkin pie spice. Makes 10 servings.

*Available at some supermarkets and specialty foods stores.

PUMPKIN PRALINE ICE CREAM PIE

I quart	**praline or butter pecan ice cream,** softened
I (9-inch)	**prepared pie shell,** baked and cooled
I cup	**canned or cooked pumpkin puree**
1/2 cup	**sugar**
1/4 teaspoon	**cinnamon**
1/4 teaspoon	**nutmeg**
1/4 teaspoon	**ginger**
2 cups	**heavy whipping cream,** divided
1/2 cup	**caramel ice cream topping**

Spread the ice cream evenly in the pie shell. Cover and freeze for 2 hours, or until firm.

Combine the pumpkin, sugar, cinnamon, nutmeg, and ginger in a large bowl and stir until well blended. In a medium bowl, whip I cup of cream until stiff peaks form. Fold the whipped cream into the pumpkin mixture. Remove pie from the freezer and spread the mixture evenly over the top. Cover and freeze for 2 hours, or until firm.

Remove pie from the freezer 15 minutes before serving, and drizzle it evenly with the caramel sauce. Whip the remaining I cup cream until stiff peaks form. Cut the pie and garnish each slice with a generous amount of whipped cream. Makes 8 servings.

PUMPKIN CRUNCH CHEESECAKE

1 $^3/_4$ cups	**crushed shortbread cookies**
I tablespoon	**butter or margarine,** melted
3 packages (8 ounces each)	**cream cheese,** softened
1 $^1/_4$ cups	**packed dark brown sugar**
I can (15 ounces) or 1 $^7/_8$ cups	**cooked pumpkin puree**
I can (5 ounces)	**evaporated milk**
2	**eggs**
2 tablespoons	**cornstarch**
$^1/_2$ teaspoon	**cinnamon**
$^1/_4$ teaspoon	**ginger**
I cup	**toffee bits**
I container (8 ounces)	**sour cream,** at room temperature
2 tablespoons	**sugar**
$^1/_2$ teaspoon	**vanilla**
$^1/_3$ cup	**caramel ice cream topping**

Preheat oven to 350 degrees. In a small bowl, combine cookie crumbs and butter. Press into bottom and I inch up the side of a 9-inch springform pan. Bake for 7 minutes (do not allow to brown). Cool on wire rack for 10 minutes.

In a large bowl, beat cream cheese and brown sugar until creamy, about 2 minutes. Add pumpkin, milk, eggs, cornstarch, cinnamon, and ginger; beat well. Pour into crust. Bake until edge is set but center still moves slightly, about 60 minutes. Remove from oven and sprinkle with toffee bits. In a small bowl, combine the sour cream, sugar, and vanilla; mix well. Spread over warm cheesecake and return to the oven. Bake for 8 minutes. Cool in pan on wire rack to room temperature. Refrigerate for at least 3 hours, or until filling is firm. Remove springform pan side and drizzle with caramel topping just before serving. Makes 10 servings.

DECADENT PUMPKIN BUTTER CAKE

1 box (18.25 ounces)	**yellow cake mix**
2 cups	**butter or margarine,** melted, divided
4	**eggs**
1 can (15 ounces) or 1⅞ cups	**cooked pumpkin puree**
8 ounces	**cream cheese,** softened
1 teaspoon	**vanilla**
1 pound	**powdered sugar**
1½ teaspoons	**pumpkin pie spice**

Preheat oven to 350 degrees and prepare a 9 x 13-inch cake pan with nonstick cooking spray.

In a large bowl, combine the cake mix, 1 cup melted butter, and 1 egg; stir until blended. Pat mixture evenly into the bottom of prepared cake pan.

In a large bowl, beat the pumpkin and cream cheese until smooth. Add the remaining 3 eggs, vanilla, and remaining 1 cup butter; stir until smooth. Add the powdered sugar and pie spice, and stir until well blended. Spread the mixture over cake mix batter. Bake until edges are lightly browned (center will not be completely set), about 40–50 minutes. Cool for 10 minutes and cut in squares. Makes 12 servings.

PUMPKIN ROLL

³/₄ cup	**flour**
¹/₂ teaspoon	**baking powder**
¹/₂ teaspoon	**baking soda**
1 teaspoon	**pumpkin pie spice**
¹/₄ teaspoon	**salt**
1 cup	**sugar**
3	**eggs**
²/₃ cup	**canned or cooked pumpkin puree**
8 ounces	**cream cheese,** softened
6 tablespoons	**butter or margarine,** softened
1 cup	**powdered sugar,** plus extra for garnish
1 teaspoon	**vanilla**

Preheat oven to 375 degrees. Line a 10 x 15-inch jelly roll pan with parchment paper and prepare the paper with nonstick cooking spray.

In a small bowl, whisk together the flour, baking powder, baking soda, pie spice, and salt. In a large bowl, combine the sugar and eggs and beat until thickened, about 2 minutes. Add the pumpkin and mix to combine. Fold in the flour mixture until combined; spread batter evenly in the prepared pan. Bake for 13–15 minutes, or until the top of the cake springs back when lightly pressed. Remove cake from oven, run a spatula around the sides of the pan to loosen, and turn it out onto a clean dish towel; peel off parchment paper. Starting with the shorter end, carefully roll up the cake with the towel and place the rolled cake on a wire rack seam-side down; cool to room temperature.

In a medium bowl, combine the cream cheese and butter and beat until smooth. Add the powdered sugar and vanilla; beat until smooth. Carefully unroll the cake and spread evenly with cream cheese filling. Re-roll the cake, wrap in aluminum foil, and refrigerate for at least 1 hour. To serve, sprinkle cake with powdered sugar and cut in 1 ¹/₄-inch slices. Makes 8 servings.

PUMPKIN DUMP CAKE

2 cans (15 ounces each) or 3³⁄₄ cups	**cooked pumpkin puree**
1 cup	**sugar**
1 can (12 ounces)	**evaporated milk**
3	**eggs**
1 tablespoon	**pumpkin pie spice**
¹⁄₂ teaspoon	**salt**
1 box (18.25 ounces)	**yellow cake mix**
1 cup	**chopped pecans**
³⁄₄ cup	**butter or margarine,** melted

Preheat oven to 350 degrees and prepare a 9 x 13-inch cake pan with nonstick cooking spray.

In a large bowl, combine the pumpkin, sugar, evaporated milk, eggs, pie spice, and salt; beat well. Pour mixture into prepared pan and sprinkle cake mix evenly over the top. Sprinkle with the pecans, and drizzle evenly with the melted butter. Bake until lightly browned, about 50–60 minutes. Makes 16 servings.

PUMPKIN POUND CAKE

1 1/2 cups	**flour**
1/2 teaspoon	**cinnamon**
1/2 teaspoon	**salt**
1/2 teaspoon	**baking soda**
1/2 teaspoon	**baking powder**
1/4 teaspoon	**cloves**
1/4 teaspoon	**nutmeg**
1 1/2 cups	**sugar**
1/2 cup	**vanilla yogurt**
3	**egg whites**
1 cup	**canned or cooked pumpkin puree**

Preheat oven to 350 degrees and prepare a 9 x 5-inch loaf pan with nonstick cooking spray.

In a medium bowl, whisk together the flour, cinnamon, salt, baking soda, baking powder, cloves, and nutmeg; reserve.

In a large bowl, combine the sugar, yogurt, and egg whites. Whisk thoroughly until blended. Add the pumpkin and stir until blended. Add the flour mixture to the pumpkin mixture and stir just until incorporated.

Pour the batter into prepared pan and bake until a toothpick inserted into the center comes out clean, about 60 minutes. Cool on a wire rack. Makes 8 servings.

PUMPKIN CRUMB CAKE

1/2 cup plus 6 tablespoons	**butter or margarine,** softened
3/4 cup	**old-fashioned oats**
2 1/4 cups	**flour,** divided
1/2 cup	**packed light brown sugar**
1/2 teaspoon	**cinnamon**
1 1/2 teaspoons	**pumpkin pie spice**
1 teaspoon	**baking soda**
1 teaspoon	**baking powder**
3/4 teaspoon	**salt**
1 1/4 cups	**sugar**
3 large	**eggs**
1 cup	**canned or cooked pumpkin puree**
1 teaspoon	**vanilla**
1/3 cup	**milk**
3/4 cup	**chopped walnuts,** optional

Preheat oven to 350 degrees and prepare an 8 x 8-inch baking dish with nonstick cooking spray.

Melt 6 tablespoons of butter in a small saucepan; cool and reserve. In a food processor or blender, pulse together oats, 1/2 cup flour, brown sugar, and cinnamon. Drizzle in the melted butter until combined; mixture will be crumbly.

In a medium bowl, whisk together 1 3/4 cups flour, pie spice, baking soda, baking powder, and salt. In a large bowl, combine 1/2 cup butter and sugar; beat until smooth. Beat in the eggs, one at a time. Add the pumpkin and vanilla and stir to combine. Gradually beat the flour mixture into the batter. Slowly add the milk and stir in the walnuts, if using. Transfer the batter to the prepared pan and sprinkle evenly with the crumb mixture. Bake until a toothpick inserted in the center comes out clean, about 55 minutes. Cool to room temperature and cut in squares. Makes 9 servings.

PUMPKIN CHOCOLATE CHIP CAKE

1 box (18.25 ounces)	**spice cake mix**
2 teaspoons	**baking soda**
2	**eggs**
1/4 cup	**water**
1 can (15 ounces) or 1 7/8 cups	**cooked pumpkin puree**
1 package (16 ounces)	**chocolate chips**

Preheat oven to 350 degrees. Prepare a 10-inch Bundt pan with nonstick cooking spray and dust with flour.

In a large bowl, whisk together cake mix with baking soda. Add eggs, water, and pumpkin; stir until well blended. Stir in chocolate chips. Pour into prepared pan and bake until a toothpick inserted in the center comes out clean, about 45 minutes. Cool on a wire rack for 10 minutes. Remove from pan and cool completely. Makes 10 servings.

CREAMY PUMPKIN TIRAMISU

1 1/2 cups	**chilled whipping cream**
3/4 cup	**sugar**
8 ounces	**mascarpone cheese,** softened
1 can (15 ounces) or 1 7/8 cups	**cooked pumpkin puree**
3/4 teaspoon	**pumpkin pie spice**
2 packages (3 ounces each)	**ladyfingers,** halved
4 tablespoons	**apple cider,** divided
4	**finely crushed gingersnap cookies**

In a large bowl beat whipping cream and sugar until peaks form. Add cheese, pumpkin, and pie spice; beat just until filling is smooth.

Line the bottom of 9-inch-diameter springform pan with 2 3/4-inch-high sides with 1 package ladyfingers, overlapping to fit. Sprinkle with 2 tablespoons apple cider. Spread half the filling over ladyfingers. Repeat a second layer with remaining package of ladyfingers, remaining 2 tablespoons apple cider, and remaining filling. Smooth. Cover and refrigerate for at least 4 hours or overnight.

To unmold, run knife around inside edge of pan. Release pan sides and sprinkle with crushed gingersnaps. Makes 8 servings.

PUMPKIN APPLE CRISP

2	**small Granny Smith apples,** peeled and chopped
³/₄ cup plus 2 tablespoons	**flour,** divided
³/₄ cup	**packed brown sugar**
³/₄ teaspoon	**pumpkin pie spice,** divided
¹/₄ cup	**butter or margarine,** softened
I cup	**canned or cooked pumpkin puree**
¹/₃ cup	**sugar**
¹/₄ cup	**milk**
I	**egg**
	whipped cream

Preheat oven to 350 degrees.

Spread apples evenly in a 9-inch glass pie plate. Microwave, uncovered, on high power until apples are barely tender, about 4–6 minutes.

In a small bowl, whisk together ³/₄ cup flour, brown sugar, and ¹/₄ teaspoon pie spice. Cut in the butter with two forks until mixture is crumbly; reserve.

In a medium bowl, combine the pumpkin, sugar, milk, egg, 2 tablespoons flour, and ¹/₂ teaspoon pie spice; stir until smooth. Pour mixture over apples, and sprinkle evenly with the reserved brown sugar mixture. Bake 30–35 minutes, or until golden brown and set. Cool 20 minutes. Serve warm with whipped cream. Makes 6 servings.

PUMPKIN CREAM PUFFS

1 cup	**water**
1/2 cup	**butter or margarine**
1 cup	**flour**
4	**eggs**
2 cups	**chilled heavy cream**
8 ounces	**cream cheese,** softened
1 cup	**canned or cooked pumpkin puree**
1/2 teaspoon	**maple flavoring**
1 cup	**powdered sugar**
2 teaspoons	**pumpkin pie spice**

Preheat oven to 400 degrees.

In large saucepan over medium-high heat, combine water and butter and bring to a rolling boil. Stir in flour; reduce heat to low. Stir vigorously over low heat about 1 minute, or until mixture forms a ball; remove from heat. Beat in eggs, all at once and continue beating until smooth.

On an ungreased baking sheet, drop dough by rounded tablespoonfuls, about 3 inches apart. Bake until puffed and golden, 20–23 minutes. Cool on pan away from draft, about 30 minutes.

In a medium bowl, whip cream until medium peaks form; reserve. In a large bowl, combine the cream cheese, pumpkin, and maple flavoring; beat until blended. Add the powdered sugar and pie spice and beat until smooth. Fold in the reserved whipped cream.

Cut off top third of each puff and pull out any strands of soft dough. Fill puffs with filling and replace tops. Makes about 24 cream puffs.

PUMPKIN BREAD PUDDING

6–8	**large croissants,** toasted and cut in 1-inch cubes to make 10 cups
2 cups	**half-and-half**
1 can (15 ounces) or 1⅞ cups	**cooked pumpkin puree**
1 cup	**firmly packed dark brown sugar**
4	**eggs**
1 teaspoon	**vanilla**
1½ teaspoons	**pumpkin pie spice**
1 cup	**golden raisins**
1 cup	**chopped pecans or walnuts,** optional
	vanilla ice cream

Preheat oven to 350 degrees and prepare a 9 x 13-inch baking dish with nonstick cooking spray; reserve.

Spread the croissant cubes on a large baking sheet and bake, turning once, for 10 minutes. Cool on the pan to room temperature and transfer cubes to a large bowl; reserve.

In a medium bowl, combine half-and-half, pumpkin, brown sugar, eggs, vanilla, and pie spice; stir until well combined. Pour the mixture over the croissant cubes and stir gently to coat. Let stand for 30 minutes, stirring occasionally. Add the raisins and nuts, if using, and stir to combine. Transfer to prepared baking dish and bake until a toothpick inserted in the center comes out clean, about 35–40 minutes. Cool on a rack for 10 minutes. Cut in squares and serve with vanilla ice cream. Makes 10 servings.

LUSCIOUS LAYERED PUMPKIN DESSERT

25	**gingersnaps,** finely crushed (about 1 1/3 cups)
1/4 cup	**butter or margarine,** melted
2 cups	**cream cheese,** softened
1/2 cup	**sugar**
1 1/2 cups	**canned or cooked pumpkin puree**
1 tablespoon	**pumpkin pie spice**
2	**eggs**
2 boxes (3.4 ounces each)	**vanilla instant pudding mix**
2 cups	**cold milk**
1 tub (8 ounces)	**frozen whipped topping,** thawed, divided
1/2 cup	**chopped toasted pecans**

Preheat oven to 350 degrees.

In a small bowl, mix together cookie crumbs and melted butter; press into bottom of a 9 x 13-inch baking dish. Bake for 10 minutes; reserve.

In a large bowl, combine the cream cheese and sugar and beat until blended. Add pumpkin and pie spice; mix well. Add eggs, 1 at a time, beating after each addition until just blended. Pour mixture over cooled crust and bake until center is almost set, about 30 minutes. Cool on a rack to room temperature.

In a large bowl, combine pudding mix and milk and beat until well blended. Add 1 cup of whipped topping and fold gently to combine. Spread pudding mixture evenly over cooked pumpkin mixture and refrigerate until firm, about 3 hours. Spread remaining whipped topping evenly over top and refrigerate for 1 more hour. Sprinkle with nuts before serving. Makes 12 servings.

MINI PUMPKIN TURNOVERS

1 cup	**canned or cooked pumpkin puree**
1/4 cup	**packed brown sugar**
1 tablespoon	**pumpkin pie spice**
1/4 teaspoon	**salt**
1 package (17.3 ounces)	**frozen puff pastry (2 sheets),** thawed
1/2 cup	**powdered sugar**
1/4 teaspoon	**maple flavoring**
2–3 teaspoons	**milk**

Preheat oven to 350 degrees and line 2 baking sheets with parchment paper.

Mix pumpkin, brown sugar, and pie spice in a small bowl.

On a lightly floured surface, roll each sheet of pastry in a 12 x 12-inch square and cut into 9, 3 x 4-inch squares. Spoon about 1 tablespoon of the pumpkin mixture in the center of each pastry square. Wet edges with water and fold over diagonally to make a triangle, pinching edges together. Arrange on prepared baking sheets, about 1 inch apart. Bake until pastry is golden brown, about 15 minutes.

In a small bowl, combine the powdered sugar, maple flavoring, and milk; stir until smooth. Remove turnovers from the oven and cool on a wire rack on the pans for 10 minutes. Drizzle the icing over the warm turnovers, remove to a wire rack and cool completely. Makes 18 turnovers.

COOKIES
AND BARS

PUMPKIN CHOCOLATE CHIP COOKIES

1 cup	**butter or margarine,** softened
³/₄ cup	**sugar**
³/₄ cup	**packed brown sugar**
1	**egg**
1 teaspoon	**vanilla**
2 cups	**flour**
1 cup	**quick-cooking oats**
1 teaspoon	**baking soda**
1 teaspoon	**cinnamon**
1 cup	**canned or cooked pumpkin puree**
1¹/₂ cups	**semisweet chocolate chips**

Preheat oven to 350 degrees and prepare 2 baking sheets with nonstick cooking spray.

In a large bowl, combine the butter, sugar, and brown sugar, and beat until light and fluffy. Add egg and vanilla and beat until smooth.

In a medium bowl, whisk together the flour, oats, baking soda, and cinnamon. Stir the flour mixture gradually into the butter mixture, alternately with the pumpkin puree, beating well after each addition. Fold in chocolate chips.

Drop by tablespoonfuls onto prepared baking sheets. Bake for 12–13 minutes, or until edges are barely browned. Remove to wire racks to cool. Makes about 50 cookies.

MAPLE-GLAZED
PUMPKIN OATMEAL COOKIES

1/2 cup	**butter or margarine,** melted
1/2 cup	**canned or cooked pumpkin puree**
1/2 cup	**packed dark brown sugar**
1/4 cup	**sugar**
1 1/2 teaspoons	**pumpkin pie spice**
1 cup	**quick-cooking oats**
1 cup	**flour**
2 teaspoons	**baking powder**
1 teaspoon	**baking soda**
1/2 teaspoon	**salt**
1/2 cup	**white chocolate morsels**
1 cup	**powdered sugar**
2 teaspoons	**maple syrup**
2 teaspoons	**milk**

Preheat oven to 350 degrees and line a baking sheet with parchment paper.

In a large bowl, combine the butter, pumpkin, brown sugar, sugar, and pie spice; stir well until blended. In a medium bowl, whisk together the oats, flour, baking powder, baking soda, and salt. Mix until blended. Add to the pumpkin mixture and stir until combined. Stir in the white chocolate morsels.

Drop cookies by rounded tablespoons on prepared baking sheet. Bake until lightly browned, about 13–16 minutes. Remove from oven and cool on a wire rack to room temperature.

In a small bowl, whisk together the powdered sugar, maple syrup, and milk. Drizzle each cookie with the icing and allow to set for 30 minutes. Makes about 24 cookies.

PUMPKIN SNICKERDOODLES

1 1/4 cups	**sugar,** divided
2 teaspoons	**pumpkin pie spice,** divided
2 teaspoons	**cinnamon**
1/2 cup	**butter or margarine,** softened
1/2 cup	**shortening**
1/2 cup	**packed light brown sugar**
3/4 cup	**canned or cooked pumpkin puree**
2 teaspoons	**vanilla**
2 3/4 cups	**flour**
1 1/2 teaspoons	**cream of tartar**
1 teaspoon	**baking soda**
1/4 teaspoon	**baking powder**
1/4 teaspoon	**salt**

In a small bowl, combine 1/4 cup sugar, 1 teaspoon pie spice, and cinnamon; stir to blend. Reserve.

In a large bowl, combine the butter, shortening, 1 cup sugar, and brown sugar, and beat until light and fluffy. Add the pumpkin and vanilla and mix until thoroughly combined.

In a medium bowl, whisk together the flour, cream of tartar, baking soda, baking powder, 1 teaspoon pie spice, and salt. Gradually add flour mixture to pumpkin mixture, stirring until well combined. Refrigerate dough for 30 minutes.

Preheat oven to 375 degrees and line a baking sheet with parchment paper.

Remove dough from refrigerator and roll in 1-inch balls; toss in cinnamon-sugar mixture before arranging on prepared baking sheet. Bake until edges are barely brown, 8–9 minutes. Cool cookies for 2 minutes on baking sheet before transferring to cooling rack. Makes about 5 dozen cookies.

PUMPKIN TOFFEE BLONDIES

3	**eggs**
$^1/_2$ cup	**Greek yogurt**
$^3/_4$ cup	**packed brown sugar**
$1^1/_2$ cups	**canned or cooked pumpkin puree**
1 teaspoon	**vanilla**
$1^1/_2$ cups	**flour**
1 teaspoon	**baking powder**
$^1/_2$ teaspoon	**baking soda**
$^1/_2$ teaspoon	**cinnamon**
$^1/_4$ teaspoon	**salt**
1 cup	**toffee bits**
	caramel ice cream topping

Preheat oven to 350 degrees and prepare a 9 x 13-inch baking dish with nonstick cooking spray.

In a large bowl, whisk together the eggs, yogurt, and brown sugar until well blended. Add the pumpkin and vanilla and stir until combined.

In a medium bowl, whisk together the flour, baking powder, baking soda, cinnamon, and salt until well combined. Add the flour mixture to the pumpkin mixture and stir until blended. Fold in the toffee bits and spread batter in the prepared baking dish. Bake for 40 minutes, or until edges are just beginning to brown and a toothpick inserted in the center comes out clean. Cool on a wire rack for 10 minutes and cut in bars. Makes 24 bars.

PUMPKIN GINGERSNAPS

$^1/_2$ cup	**butter or margarine,** softened
1 cup	**sugar,** plus extra for rolling the cookies
$^1/_2$ cup	**canned or cooked pumpkin puree**
$^1/_4$ cup	**molasses**
1	**egg**
1 teaspoon	**vanilla**
2 $^1/_3$ cups	**flour**
2 teaspoons	**baking soda**
2 teaspoons	**cinnamon**
1 $^1/_2$ teaspoons	**ginger**
$^1/_2$ teaspoon	**cloves**
$^1/_2$ teaspoon	**salt**

In a large bowl, combine the butter and sugar and beat until creamy. Add the pumpkin, molasses, egg, and vanilla, and mix until well combined.

In a medium bowl, whisk together flour, baking soda, cinnamon, ginger, cloves, and salt. Add the flour mixture to the pumpkin mixture and stir until combined. Cover the bowl and refrigerate the dough for at least 1 hour.

Preheat oven to 350 degrees and line a baking sheet with parchment paper.

Fill a small bowl with sugar. Roll dough in 1$^1/_2$-inch balls and coat with the sugar before arranging on prepared baking sheet, about 2 inches apart. Bake until cookies are set at the edges and cracked but still soft, about 10–13 minutes. Cool on a wire rack. Makes about 36 cookies.

PUMPKIN SHORTBREAD COOKIES

2 1/4 cups	**flour**
1/4 teaspoon	**salt**
1 teaspoon	**pumpkin pie spice**
1 3/4 sticks	**butter or margarine,** softened
1/2 cup	**powdered sugar**
1/4 cup	**canned or cooked pumpkin puree**

In a medium bowl, whisk together the flour, salt, and pie spice.

In a large bowl, beat together the butter, powdered sugar, and pumpkin until creamy. Add the flour mixture and stir until combined but still crumbly. Use hands to press mixture together. Cover and refrigerate for 30 minutes.

Preheat oven to 325 degrees, and prepare an 8 x 8-inch baking dish with nonstick cooking spray.

Press the dough into the dish and prick the top with a fork in 2 x 2-inch squares. Bake 30–35 minutes, or until lightly browned. Cool for 5 minutes before removing from pan. Carefully cut in squares while still warm. Makes 16 servings.

PUMPKIN MINI WHOOPIE PIES

2 cups	**flour**
1 teaspoon	**baking powder**
1 teaspoon	**baking soda**
1 $^1/_2$ teaspoons	**cinnamon,** divided
$^1/_2$ teaspoon	**ginger**
$^1/_2$ teaspoon	**salt**
10 tablespoons	**butter or margarine,** softened, divided
1 $^1/_4$ cups	**sugar**
2	**eggs,** lightly beaten
1 cup	**canned or cooked pumpkin puree**
1 $^1/_2$ teaspoons	**vanilla,** divided
4 ounces	**cream cheese,** softened
1 $^1/_2$ cups	**powdered sugar**

Preheat oven to 350 degrees. Line 4 baking sheets with parchment paper.

In a medium bowl, whisk together flour, baking powder, baking soda, 1 teaspoon cinnamon, ginger, and salt. In a large bowl, combine 4 tablespoons butter and sugar; beat for 2 minutes until creamy. Beat in eggs, one at a time. Add pumpkin and vanilla; beat until smooth. Add the flour mixture and stir until combined. Drop by heaping measuring teaspoons onto prepared baking sheets. Bake for 10–13 minutes, or until springy to the touch. Cool for 5 minutes; remove to wire racks to cool completely.

In a medium bowl, combine the cream cheese, 6 tablespoons butter, $^1/_2$ teaspoon vanilla, and $^1/_2$ teaspoon cinnamon; beat until smooth. Gradually beat in powdered sugar until light and fluffy. Spread a heaping teaspoon of cream cheese mixture on the flat side of one cookie; top with second cookie. Repeat. Store, covered, in refrigerator. Makes about 36 whoopie pies.

PUMPKIN
GINGER 6-LAYER BARS

2 cups	**gingersnap crumbs**
$1/2$ cup	**butter or margarine,** melted
I can (14 ounces)	**sweetened condensed milk**
$3/4$ cup	**canned or cooked, pumpkin puree**
I teaspoon	**cinnamon**
$1/4$ teaspoon	**nutmeg**
$3/4$ cup	**white chocolate chips**
$3/4$ cup	**butterscotch chips**
I cup	**pecans,** coarsely chopped
$1 1/2$ cups	**sweetened shredded coconut**

Preheat oven to 350 degrees. Line an 8 x 8-inch pan with aluminum foil, leaving I inch of overhang on two sides. Prepare with nonstick cooking spray.

In a small bowl, combine the gingersnap crumbs and melted butter and stir until well blended. Press mixture evenly in bottom of pan. In another small bowl, combine condensed milk, pumpkin, cinnamon, and nutmeg and stir until blended. Pour mixture over gingersnap crust.

Sprinkle evenly with white chocolate chips, followed by butterscotch chips, pecans, and coconut. Bake for 25–35 minutes, or until coconut is lightly browned. Cool in pan to room temperature and refrigerate until firm. Use foil to lift bars from pan and cut in 2-inch squares. Makes 16 bars.

PUMPKIN BARS WITH CREAM CHEESE FROSTING

4	**eggs**
1²/₃ cups	**sugar**
1 cup	**vegetable oil**
1 can (15 ounces) or 1⅞ cups	**cooked pumpkin puree**
2 cups	**flour**
2 teaspoons	**cinnamon**
2 teaspoons	**baking powder**
1 teaspoon	**baking soda**
1 teaspoon	**salt**
½ teaspoon	**ginger**
8 ounces	**cream cheese,** softened
½ cup	**butter or margarine,** softened
1 teaspoon	**vanilla**
2 cups	**powdered sugar**

Preheat oven to 325 degrees and prepare a 9 x 12-inch baking pan with nonstick cooking spray.

In a large bowl, combine the eggs, sugar, oil, and pumpkin; beat until light and fluffy. In a medium bowl, whisk together the flour, cinnamon, baking powder, baking soda, salt, and ginger. Add the flour mixture to the pumpkin mixture and mix until thoroughly combined and smooth. Spread batter in the prepared pan and bake for 45–50 minutes, or until a toothpick inserted in the center comes out clean. Cool to room temperature.

In a medium bowl, beat together the cream cheese, butter, and vanilla until smooth. Add the powdered sugar and mix until combined. Spread the frosting evenly over the bars and cut in 1½ x 3-inch rectangles. Makes 24 bars.

PUMPKIN PECAN PIE BARS

1 cup	**flour**
1/2 cup	**quick-cooking oats**
1 cup	**packed dark brown sugar,** divided
10 tablespoons	**butter or margarine,** softened, divided
3/4 teaspoon	**salt,** divided
1 can (15 ounces) or 1 7/8 cups	**cooked pumpkin puree**
1 can (11 ounces)	**evaporated milk**
2	**eggs**
3/4 cup	**sugar**
1 teaspoon	**vanilla**
2 teaspoons	**pumpkin pie spice**
1/2 cup	**chopped pecans**

Preheat oven to 350 degrees and prepare a 9 x 13-inch baking pan with nonstick cooking spray.

In a large bowl, combine the flour, oats, 1/2 cup brown sugar, 8 tablespoons butter, and 1/4 teaspoon salt. Stir until combined (mixture will be crumbly) and press into prepared pan. Bake for 15 minutes; transfer pan to a wire rack and cool.

In a medium bowl, combine the pumpkin, evaporated milk, eggs, sugar, vanilla, 1/2 teaspoon salt, and pie spice; beat well. Pour into cooled crust and bake for 20 minutes.

In a small bowl, combine the pecans, 1/2 cup brown sugar, 2 tablespoons butter; sprinkle over pumpkin filling. Return to oven and bake 15–20 minutes, or until filling is set. Cool in pan on rack and cut into bars. Makes 12 bars.

PUMPKIN
CHOCOLATE SWIRL BROWNIES

3 ounces	**cream cheese,** softened
3/4 cup plus 1 tablespoon	**butter or margarine,** softened, divided
2 3/4 cups	**sugar,** divided
5	**eggs**
1 cup	**canned or cooked pumpkin puree**
3 teaspoons	**vanilla,** divided
1/2 teaspoon	**cinnamon**
1/4 teaspoon	**ginger**
1 1/4 cups plus 1 tablespoon	**flour,** divided
3/4 teaspoon	**baking powder**
1/2 teaspoon	**salt**
6 ounces	**unsweetened baking chocolate,** chopped
1/4 cup	**milk**

Preheat oven to 325 degrees and prepare a 9 x 13-inch baking pan with nonstick cooking spray.

In a medium bowl, beat cream cheese and 1 tablespoon butter for 30 seconds. Add 1/2 cup sugar and beat to combine. Beat in 1 egg, pumpkin, 1 teaspoon vanilla, cinnamon, and ginger. Stir in 1 tablespoon flour; reserve. In a small bowl, whisk together 1 1/4 cups flour, baking powder, and salt. In a large saucepan, combine the chocolate and 3/4 cup butter. Heat until melted and smooth. Gradually add 2 1/4 cups sugar, beating just until combined. Beat in remaining 4 eggs one at a time. Add milk and 2 teaspoons vanilla. Gradually add flour mixture and stir just until combined. Spread chocolate mixture evenly in the prepared pan. Spoon cream cheese mixture in mounds on top and swirl into the chocolate batter. Bake until center is just set, about 60 minutes. Cool and cut in squares. Makes 36 brownies.

PUMPKIN GRANOLA BARS

3 $1/4$ cups	**old-fashioned oats**
1 $1/2$ teaspoons	**pumpkin pie spice**
$1/2$ teaspoon	**salt**
$1/4$ cup	**packed dark brown sugar**
1 cup	**canned or cooked pumpkin puree**
$1/2$ cup	**maple syrup**
1 teaspoon	**vanilla**
$1/2$ cup	**dried cranberries**
$1/2$ cup	**chopped walnuts**
$1/4$ cup	**pepitas* (hulled pumpkin seeds),** optional

Preheat oven to 350 degrees and prepare an 8 x 8-inch baking pan with nonstick cooking spray.

In a large bowl, combine the oats, pie spice, and salt; stir to combine.

In a medium bowl, combine the brown sugar, pumpkin, maple syrup, and vanilla; stir until well combined. Pour over the oat mixture and stir until well combined. Stir in the cranberries, walnuts, and pepitas, if using.

Press the mixture firmly into prepared baking pan. Bake until golden brown and firm, about 30–35 minutes. Cool in pan for 10 minutes. Cut into bars and cool on wire rack to room temperature. Makes 16 bars.

*Available at specialty and natural food stores.

PUMPKIN ANGEL BARS

1 box (16 ounces)	**angel food cake mix**
1 can (15 ounces) or 1 ⅞ cups	**cooked pumpkin puree**
1 ¼ teaspoons	**pumpkin pie spice,** divided
¾ cup	**powdered sugar**
1 ½ tablespoons	**hot water**
1 teaspoon	**vanilla**

Preheat oven to 350 degrees and prepare a 9 x 13-inch pan with nonstick cooking spray.

In a large bowl, combine cake mix, pumpkin, and 1 teaspoon pumpkin pie spice; stir until smooth. Spread in prepared pan and bake until top is lightly browned and a toothpick inserted in the center comes out clean, about 25–30 minutes. Transfer pan to a wire rack and cool to room temperature.

In a small bowl, beat the powdered sugar, water, vanilla, and ¼ teaspoon pie spice until combined. Drizzle over the top and allow to set for 30 minutes before cutting into bars. Makes 24 bars.

PUMPKIN BISCOTTI

3 1/2 cups	**flour**
2 teaspoons	**baking powder**
1/2 teaspoon	**salt**
2 teaspoons	**pumpkin pie spice**
2	**eggs**
1 1/2 cups	**packed light brown sugar**
1/2 cup	**canned or cooked pumpkin puree**
1 tablespoon	**vanilla**
1 1/4 cups	**chopped, toasted pecans**
1/4 cup	**melted white chocolate,**
	for drizzling or dipping

Preheat oven to 350 degrees and line a baking sheet with parchment paper. Fill a spray bottle with tepid water.

In a medium bowl, whisk together flour, baking powder, salt, and pie spice; reserve. In a large bowl, combine the eggs, brown sugar, pumpkin, and vanilla; beat until well blended, about 2 minutes. Add the flour mixture and pecans to the pumpkin mixture and stir to blend (mixture will be crumbly).

On a lightly floured surface, divide the dough in half and shape each in a 3 x 10-inch loaf. Arrange on prepared baking sheet and bake until just firm to the touch, about 25–30 minutes. Remove from oven and cool for 5 minutes.

Decrease oven temperature to 325 degrees. Use the spray bottle to moisten the top and sides of the loaves. Transfer loaves to a cutting board and use a serrated knife to cut in 1/2-inch thick slices. Arrange the slices in a single layer on the baking sheet. Bake until firm, about 20 minutes, turning slices over midway through baking. Cool on a wire rack to room temperature and drizzle with white chocolate. Makes about 36 biscotti.

PUMPKIN BUTTERSCOTCH COOKIES

2 cups	**flour**
1 1/2 teaspoons	**baking powder**
1 teaspoon	**baking soda**
1/2 teaspoon	**salt**
1 teaspoon	**cinnamon**
2	**eggs**
1 cup	**sugar**
1/2 cup	**vegetable oil**
1 cup	**canned or cooked pumpkin puree**
1 teaspoon	**vanilla**
1 cup	**butterscotch chips**

Preheat oven to 325 degrees and line 2 baking sheets with parchment paper.

In a medium bowl, whisk together the flour, baking powder, baking soda, salt, and cinnamon; reserve.

In a large bowl, beat the eggs and sugar until creamy, about 1 minute. Add the oil, pumpkin, and vanilla; mix until blended. Stir in the flour mixture until incorporated, and fold in the butterscotch chips.

Drop by heaping tablespoonfuls on prepared baking sheets, spacing cookies 2 inches apart. Bake, rotating pans once during cooking, until edges are lightly browned, about 12–14 minutes. Cool cookies on baking sheets for 5 minutes before transferring to a wire rack. Makes about 36 cookies.

NOTES

NOTES

METRIC CONVERSION CHART

Volume Measurements			Weight Measurements			Temperature Conversion	
U.S.	Metric		U.S.	Metric		Fahrenheit	Celsius
1 teaspoon	5 ml		1/2 ounce	15 g		250	120
1 tablespoon	15 ml		1 ounce	30 g		300	150
1/4 cup	60 ml		3 ounces	90 g		325	160
1/3 cup	75 ml		4 ounces	115 g		350	180
1/2 cup	125 ml		8 ounces	225 g		375	190
2/3 cup	150 ml		12 ounces	350 g		400	200
3/4 cup	175 ml		1 pound	450 g		425	220
1 cup	250 ml		2 1/4 pounds	1 kg		450	230